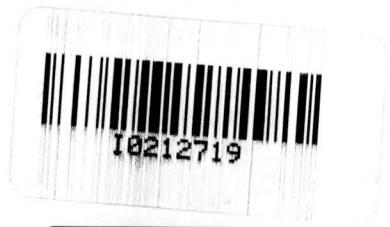

# LIFT

INSIGHTS TO ELEVATE YOUR

MIND, BODY AND SPIRIT

by

## BRIAN GERMAIN

# LIFT

## Insights to Elevate your Mind, Body and Spirit

### By Brian S. Germain

ISBN-13: 978-0-9911923-3-5

LCCN: 2025901432

# Introduction

**Why I wrote this book**

Through living my strange life, I have found my way to a uniquely resilient perspective. This viewpoint involves an uplifting, balanced way to see things, always striving to rise up to the wholistic point of view that makes sense of it all. After four decades of profoundly educational experiences while hurling myself out of perfectly good airplanes, I have learned some things about how to promote human brilliance in the face of potential catastrophe. This is the generalizable life wisdom that I wish to share with humanity in this slightly odd little book.

I have noticed that the most helpful lessons I have learned through being a teacher of parachute flight, also apply to life in general. I therefore ask your forgiveness of my over-reliance upon skydiving metaphors. I have observed that risk in general has proven for me to be one of the most profound lenses through which I have seen truth, in visceral moments of knowing. Even the misadventures that ended badly still provided more than just a painful lesson, but one that made all involved much wiser. The "disasters" inevitably led to a feeling of celebratory gratitude in our return to flight, and gave cause for the mental investment in creating a magnificent alternative to eating dirt. To fly without fear, we must love the experience of flight.

I have also realized that learning about ourselves is the inevitable result of our reaching for survival. The process of expansion is multidimensional, calling forth our evolution in every regard, and often in unexpected ways. The world shows us our inadequacies, as we bear the soft white underbellies of our insufficient level of readiness. Failure is a consequence of an incomplete formula, an insufficient understanding of the situation. Wisdom is the natural consequence of long-term survival on a dangerous planet, as it leads us to add variables to the formula, and reduce the expression to a simpler form. Having done some sixty orbits around this planet that keeps rushing up at me, and my thousands of sky-friends all over the world.

The greatest skydivers I have ever met are truly brilliant, well-rounded individuals who are genuinely happy human beings. Their success stories are partly based on their commitment to training, partly due to their capacity for flowing joy without an ounce of fear, and partly about their "Zen" way of being that keeps it all in balance. They can flow in creative motion in the vast space above our heads, powerfully execute a parachute malfunction procedure like a ninja, and then can sit quietly, soothing a worried first-jumper waiting for their airplane. They are kind, they are inspiring, and they take care of each other. That love is better than the best YouTube videos we painstakingly edit for the inspirational upliftment of humanity. The life of a skydiver is awe and beauty wrapped in courage and friendship.

*-Brian Germain, March 31, 2025*

**"Lift":** (*aerodynamics*) *the upward force that opposes weight, commonly used to prevent crashing. Metaphorically, to represent a mental force vector that increases the joy of being alive, and one's ability to stay that way.*

When I jump out of an airplane, I believe things will go well for me. I have faith in my equipment, in myself, and I surrender to trust in faith itself as a cosmological principle. I believe that if I keep my mind/body in a good feeling, with my attention focused on the way that feels best in each moment, everything is going to work out fine. I expect joy-filled flights, but I am not terribly surprised when I have an unusual situation or parachute malfunction. I just don't worry much about it; I accept it and immediately move in into my well-rehearsed emergency procedures. I know that all will go well for me, one way or another, simply because I am there. I am the pilot, and I choose my intention when I get into the cockpit; I choose to make things end well. This holistic state of mental preparation allows me to fly with joy in my heart, without fear clouding my head with its incessant vibe-wrecking paranoia. For nearly 40 years and many thousands of skydives all over the world, this attitude has served me quite well. Perhaps hearing more about this frame of mind will help you too.

Connecting to a productive mindset, for me, is about finding your way back to the enthusiastic, "yes I can" attitude that we were all born with. I call this my "Original Happiness". It is this lively perspective that allows our creative expression to flow forth, yielding brilliant adaptation in the heat of the moment. This is you, when you get your game-face on. The world needs more people with a sparkle in their eyes and a shine in their heart. This is about remembering the best version of you, your inner power. It is about *knowing* who you really are.

I believe we are best served by stepping eagerly forward into life's many challenges with a sense of adventure, empowered by a trust in the sharpness of our minds, and our surprising capacity for insight in a crisis. This is what I mean by knowing oneself. If we do not rise up into this expanded version of ourselves, we will forget who we are, and fear will make us meek. It will rob us of an empowered life, both before, during and after the deeply unpleasant experiences that fear inevitably creates.

Fear merely shows us that our perspective and our way of being was out of balance in this mindset. It is one way to see the world, a possible perspective. When we feel afraid, we are incongruent with where we actually wanted the situation to go, because we are immersed in the opposing visualization. We expected the worst, and we experienced the consequence of that frame of mind. We looked where we didn't want to go, and our thinking locked us into the unwanted outcome, rather than the desired experience. All great pilots, and those empowered by a strong mindset, notice fear, but then find a way to soothe it through thought and action. They allow themselves to become immersed in the mental flow of creating the desired experience, and are certain that they can. This is empowerment.

## Your Breath and Your Mind are One

Regardless of the context, your choice to turn the situation around begins with a repeating loop of constructive thoughts, supported by a grounded, focused feeling in the body. This starts with getting your breath under control so you can clear your mind of the momentum of the past. With a firm commitment to maintain our composure in all situations, we can remain fully conscious within the apparent chaos, a steadfast boulder in the middle of a raging river.

## A Note on Your Personal Weirdness Alarm

The river of novel realization feels weird at first. New ideas feel awkward, and our natural tendency used to be to avoid new things and questionable risks that offer necessary rewards. It requires finding your balance, your bearings, and tolerating strangeness with grace and forgiveness. It will keep showing up, the compression-turned expansion, the slowing down of the mind into the simple truth feels true. Even when a whackiest conflicts with normalcy can be embraced and released. The shock is loved for what it is, the body's natural impulses to contract in fear of the new. We must embrace the value of this moment, this lesson in an upper level lesson in your soul's degree in love. As we pursue love, we find passion and joy. We feel the truth that we belong in heaven on earth, every single one of us. And we have somehow concluded that we have work to do on our souls to find out more of what love really creates within us, through us, and beyond us. Love is everywhere, a breath to be inhaled in a moment of gentle surrender, we let love shine on our souls.

Try this when you are beginning to feel angst and feverous speed within your mind and body: Take a deep slow breath in, all the way in, and when you get to full expansion, hold. Relax into the silent space of stillness for as much time as it took to inhale your share of the sky. Then slowly, gently, release the breath. Take as much time as you did to inhale, slowly returning the sky in deep gratitude. Collect all that you are into this present moment of peaceful silence, in the infinite space created at the bottom of your breath. Awaken all of your wisdom, of all of the minds within your mind, and realize the vastness what who and what you are. Collect all that you are in the powerful realization statement: **I AM.** As you begin to inhale gently, expand outward in your awareness, to hear the fundimental nature of the universe in a single word: **ONE.**

If we can resurrect the higher perspective in the feeling of Oneness, we have access to the empowered version of our minds, the hero within. This mindset will be required for the turbulent skies of the human experience, but with an elevated perspective, the soul becomes wise through life's many unexpected challenges. Our lessons are always a polarity of oneness, desired and undesired, one informing the other. This is how humans learn. That means every mistake you ever made, every embarrassing blunder you stumbled into, instantaneously created the polar opposite realization of the desired future that would not have come into existence, had you not walked the path you walked. The humbling truth we experience sets the mind on a trajectory to dream of something better, leveraging what has been.

**Realization**

An insight that awakens a new perspective is the lift that opposes the weight of the belief that today is yesterday. It is an "aha" moment that clarifies your understanding, stemming from a passionate thought-stream within you. When you realize something deeply true and significant, you must savor the emotion of excitement, but then you must take appropriate action. When you take action on your best ideas, the world gets better in a way that you personally have created. An insight begins as an internal experience, but when we inspire others about our invigorating concept, the possibility expands on a quantum level. Through the force of our passionate will, we can conceive and create new possibilities that never existed before. This is why you are here.

All beings have this capability, because we are all insightful in our unique ways, and the epiphanies that give our lives meaning provide us emotional leverage over that which needs to be changed, improved and expanded upon. Life will naturally become some form of what we desire if we stay the course, but that is not a certainty in this treacherous world. Doubt will return when you again forget who you really are, and you will need to remember. This happens to each of us every single day. We slip into normal patterns of thought, the basic mindset, and we react to our world in semi-conscious ways, with a semi-closed mind. In our slumber, we forget our dream, or worse, we ignore it because we invest our faith in doubt. If we are to be the powerful creators we were meant to be, we must decide to awaken from the dream of disempowerment. It is a lie that we tell ourselves to keep us small and, so we subconsciously believe, safe.

If you decide right now that you are now choosing the awakened, brightly shining version of your enthusiasm, the grey times will become shorter and less often henceforth. You have to decide that from this moment forward, in this instant of realization, that you are different. You must remember the exhilarating feeling of the insight itself, the feeling of lift. The very essence of the life force is the inspired mind/body, a conscious physical being of clear intent. A mind is not just a bunch of neurons firing to create the illusion of a person. A mind is a Divine spark that does not merely interact with the world, it creates the world.

## Persistence of Faith

In order to see our visions unfold in this slowly expanding world, we must have trust in the inevitability of our creations. The shadow of our doubt creeps in and the walls of our lives get closer together. This nightmare is all based on a lie told by the human ego-mind within all of us, the physical self that is fighting to stay alive. The ego is the scared and cornered program in the minds of all humans and animals that will kill to stay alive. The ego is the separated self, an island of consciousness made present by the belief that you are this body, disconnected from the rest of humanity, apart from the natural world. This limited perspective, the small self, defined only as a frail physical body, and although it comprises a reasonably vast universe, it is nothing in comparison to the wider perspective of the larger Self, the "I Am" of it all.

The two are in conflict from a certain perspective. The ego wants to be left alone to count its money and bullets, and celebrate itself as a legend in a small mirror. The Cosmic Self seeks connection with all, and revels in harmony, joy and love. Our minds are an Odd Couple indeed, but the two are paired within us nonetheless. We are all of it, and if we are to love ourselves as a whole, in complete and unlimited acceptance, we must smile lovingly as we gently take the microphone from the Ego and hand it to the Cosmic self.

## Unlearning the Old You

In our pursuit of a vaster view that provides access to wisdom and deeper meaning, we must examine the beliefs that create limitation of the self. These are thought-forms based on a moment of mislearning. We mislearn that we are horrible at riding a bicycle when we are young, but then we forgive and release that perspective. We get back on the bike again and again, until we build the skill to ride well. We become kind to our minds in these moments of grace, and so we are able redefine our beliefs in a trusting amorphous state of not-knowing. We let our past go, in favor of a more constructive direction of focus, a more creative stream of thought.

Many of the lessons we still believe to be true are caused in moments of emotional pain in the long, drawn-out experiences of what we can call "crashing". We crystalize the mislearned ideas that we aren't good at something through repetition of the thought, and thusly cut a deep groove in our minds. The persistent negative emotion form a long term memory, a belief system left unexamined. This leaves one in an apathetic mindset of giving up, and we stop trying because of this false belief. We then temporarily stall our soul's development, and our freedom is limited, until we change our minds.

## *It is our beliefs that limit us, not the world.*

We have believed many things that we later realized to be untrue, but when we suffered the most it was because we believed in an unloving lie. Here is a lie that the ego tells us to get us into the back seat, where it feels safe: "YOU CAN'T". For injured skydivers, no return to the sky is possible without the shedding of doubt, the vile lie told by a fearful little self that doesn't know its own power. A downed pilot, by definition, feels down at least part of the time. It is simply the experience they are in for a time. In order to get our confidence flowing again, we must first accept what has occurred in the past, our role in it, and then we must forgive and become wiser than before. We are tied to the past until we learn the life lesson, but then we can let it go, as it was.

**The Lesson Yields Wisdom**

For all the oopses and ouches, there is always the cooperative counterweight represented by of their meaning. When we learn what happens when we fly our parachutes too far downwind of the trees, we get to meet the squirrels. Every time, forevermore, we will get a feeling, a powerful constant urge to stay on the upwind side of the landing area. We have learned the consequences and the memory stuck. Our tree landing was leveraged and turned into the wisdom behind the skill, and we left the squirrels behind. This is called emotional alchemy, an enlightened pivoting of the mindset.

Once we realize that we have learned, then we can then leave the feeling of crashing behind us, as we shift our attention to the joy of the flight at hand. We do not worry, but we do not ever fully slacken our awareness into complacent expectation of simplicity. Things do have a way of popping up for our intentional, adaptive maneuvering. The pilot is the mind of the aircraft, the awareness of the machine. The pilots gaze is with clear intention to open-mindedly stand ready to do what is necessary to protect and serve the passengers and if entirely possible, the aircraft; if it's not too much trouble.

Your desire to stay focused, to conscientiously guide your life's day to day endeavors and tasks, this is your leverage over the path the situation takes. The mindset you have thus far nurtured has been sufficient to cause your surprisingly persistent survival. This repeating miracle has occurred for and improbably, uncommonly long time, suggesting that more than mere luck is at hand. This was no accident; it was your consciousness looking forward to what is ahead and flying gracefully between the things around you. Each pilot, in their own mind, must seek to perceive the surrounding situation in a wholistic manner. This brilliant demonstration of human capabilities and trusting in the flying machine in this unlikely synergy demonstrating who we are as a species, and an extension of the humanness within all of us. We do not want to spend all our time on the couch where it seems so safe, we want to be in the flow of a situation in motion, alert and in time-stopping awe.

The process of collecting ones awareness again and again, in a wide-reaching wondering of what is so. What is the situation, the aviator asks. What is the airspeed and the decent rate and where is this bucket of bolts heading to at the moment? This may, or may not be where you intend to go. In some cases, the way things are going does require a refreshing of the mental cache, the Zen moment of an effective clearing of the mind, through a cleansing breath done intentionally, the pilot becomes new again. This experience is yours for the taking, to be incorporated in your life, in the differencing context of your daily experience. It still applies.

The wisdom of the deliberate reset is born from many times in my aviation career that I experienced the natural consequences in not following a feeling to zig or zag, and it has taught me time and again, slow down and breath your mind to a stop as often as possible. If things feel dicey above the yellow line, it is time to pack up and go home. Go big or go home only works if you are fully feeling it. Rather than regret the many ways we learned these lessons, we can simply note the bump in understanding, and in our minds simply say, "check". Now you can let it go and the fear that you won't remember that specific gem of truth. You must trust that you will. Faith is an integral aspect of wisdom. Trust in the truth.

## Radical Acceptance

I have found in the healing process, the victim mindset is going to show up as a natural component, and the fearful doubt often consumes us for a time. This truth must be accepted so it can be forgiven. I have also found that a mind set in motion with dedicated conviction can change the course of history. This also must be accepted. Embrace all that led to this reality in which you find yourself, and do not sidestep your own influence in unwanted events coming to pass. You had an impact, with your response to the situation, you influenced reality. In that moment, when you zigged when you should have zagged, you didn't have the right mindset to create an experience to your liking. Accept this. It was you. Making excuses and seeking to blame others for our failures to make our experience tolerable is more than a waste of your time, it is a distraction from the reality that you were at the center of everything that happens in your life. Our disempowerment is based on an untruth, an illusion created within the mind.

## The Resilient Knowing of Self

You are free to believe in yourself as a freedom-seeking being of unlimited creativity and power, who exists as the conceptual high-water mark of your most valiant moments. That is one possible mindset. Another version of your mind will see every failure as conclusive proof of your incompetence, your lack of intelligence, and your weakness. This thought-stream will create more experiences that validate this as a seeming truth. Everybody has those moments, when we are so angry at ourselves for making the wrong choice in life. Without confronting and evicting these false beliefs, they will continue to create our personal reality in a mirroring way. We must deliberately and ritualistically put the past behind us so it does not become us. The past isn't who you are, it was what you did.

If a skydiver has a hard landing, they must learn from it. They must remember what it looked like in the seconds leading to that one painful experience, but then a they must spend the rest of their lives visualizing the alternative flow of the experience. One of the days that helped me to become a better pilot was a windy cold day in March in northern Vermont. In a naive jaunt into risk, I launched my experimental paraglider into very windy conditions in the early spring of 1993. I immediately discovered this to be a huge mistake, as the upslope breeze lifted me vertically above the mountain, and backward toward the turbulence on the downwind side of the tree-covered hill. I pulled

17

together my skills, and managed to push forward to the landing area on the upwind side of the mountain, but then my paraglider collapsed. I fell from approximately 100 feet, and performed the best ninja roll I could muster, but it was not quite enough.

The orthopedic surgeon who bolted and screwed me back together had some bad news for me. He told me that I was never going to jump again. In fact, he said with kind sad eyes, I would probably never walk properly again. I took a deep breath in silence, considering what was said. Then I remembered something. I remembered who I am. In a moment of renewed inspiration, I said, "Doc, I appreciate that you don't want to get my hopes too high for fear that I will be disappointed, but with all due respect, you don't know me". Two and a half years later I went back to Dr. Andrew Kaplan and presented him with a signed, framed picture of me in freefall at sunrise. I then told him that I had just won the X-Games in Freefly Skydiving, I was the World Champion. To a determined mind unwilling to surrender, miracles are indeed possible.

We have all thought ourselves a hopeless failure at one point or another. We can then linger in cold judgment of ourselves and limit our vision for what is possible. In doing so we split of our world in two, with our home on the other side of the chasm of our judgment. The certainty of our failure is our own sledgehammer of "truth" to wield, if we choose to tell our story that way. If we continue to beat ourselves over the head with our self-abusive, repeated memories of unwanted tragedies, we kindle a fire within our minds that burns our dreams. It is up to us to stop these mind-fires, and our higher self can rise up out of the ashes. If we decide to forgive and stop looping the story, we can expand beyond it, because of it. Life does not happen to us; it happens for us.

A sustainable positive outlook is based on an internal decision to be buoyant in all moments. What all of us come to realize, sooner or later, is that our happiness is not derived from attainments, accomplishments or circumstances, but experiences entirely within ourselves. Conditions ebb and flow, and aspects of what occurs will always be out of your control. Things don't always go the way you pictured in your mind, and people don't always say what you wish they would to make you happy. They are tasked with voicing their perspective, not yours. Therefore, we realize that our happiness is something we can and must conjure on our own, regardless of the context. Your uplifting perspective is a choice, a perennial affirmation that you have what it takes, no matter what others expect or how much it hurts to face the contrasting doubt of those who have not seen and do not believe. Life doesn't give us what we deserve, it gives us what we expect, and we must expect more brightly.

## An Adaptable Mindset

One of the key lessons we have realized is about adaptability of mindset. A new perspective may strain the eyes at first, but with soothing breathing, adaptation can occur. Back in the 1990's, some of us decided to learn how to fly straight down in freefall, head toward the planet, spine parallel to the wind-flow. When we begin flying headfirst, it feels upside down. Then we adapt and make this feel normal. We then went on to explore the 5th dimensional world of "freeflying", combining both head up and head down orientations, and we made that feel normal too.

At the beginning of the awakening journey, the flip of perspective continues to make the new worldview a confusing time of adjustment, but we learn to adapt. Just as it feels wrong at first to be upside down, so too, is the shift of perspective to a cosmology of Oneness, and the knowing that all is either love, or a call to love. This period of adjustment takes as long as it takes, but it is ultimately and open-mindedness of the soul which allows all orientations to feel normal so that grace can flow at all times. Resistance to what is, is no more. Thusly, the wise searcher of deeper meaning is mentally flexible and full of the grace of wonder. The ever-widening mind is a vaster container for truth of an uncommon nature.

Things will flip and spin around and we must have the ability to not judge what we see as anything but what it is. No labels serve the flexible mind, because judgment is the closing of a mind, not the opening of a heart. It is this opening that allows for new information about the world, and about ourselves. Wonder is the sublime sensation of the awakening mind connected to its knowing of itself; eager and curious about potential expansion of knowing more about who one truly is at heart.

To know oneself, one must learn from our clarifying experiences. In my life, the wisdom of self is clarified through exploring the metaphorical relationship between the dream of flight and the fear of crashing. All the stunts that I did not land, all those moments when I didn't carry the vibe, that alternative created an equal and opposite force called joyful gratitude for things going so well next time. Appreciation can be magnified by comparisons, shit to shine as it were, as two magnetic poles of the same system. Through the examination of these experiences, we clarify what is preferred, and so become more aware of our strengths and current weaknesses, and we form a better flight plan next time.

## The Quantum Physics of Flight

I have, at all times, two inseparable goals as a teacher of flight. The first is to keep others from crashing. The second goal is to nurture the love of flight; to make way for transcendent moments in the sky that last forever. If the first goal is not achieved, the second is clearly not on the table. If a skydiver is preoccupied with "not crashing", they do not explore all that flight has to teach us. This mindset misses the whole point. Further, our skills are eventually found wanting when we do not try new things, and wiggle our way into new skill over time. It is indeed a harrowing path to play with a parachute like a toy, but if you don't experience all the possibilities with a brave sense of adventure, one will certainly fall short of a mark that matters. It is these intertwined agendas, surviving and thriving, that alternately fill our time as skydiving instructors. I believe this to be true for the whole of the human experience.

You must wonder about what might go wrong so that you can wonder about, and rehearse, the appropriate solutions. We practice cutting away the main parachute and pulling the reserve quite frequently. If we don't, we are likely to experience and error in execution. Alternatively, if we practice malfunctions procedures too often, something quite different happens. We experience Quantum physics in action. The observer effects the observed in a profound way. The building blocks of what we think of as matter, and the light in which it exists, does not actually adhere to the Newtonian principles in which we have felt so safe and sane within for so very long. This new model of physics, based on the work of a great many geniuses of our species, shows us that that you matter.

Matter itself is not solid at all, but a swarm of energy potentialities. It exists as possibilities super-positioned equally across the quantum field of what we call the material world. In walks consciousness, the observer with a point of view, and in our case, an opinion. This expectational projection of the observer can be one of worrying about a crash, or the graceful flight of a talented canopy pilot making magic happen. Your mind is creating your own private Universe, based on your expectations.

This is not to say that the consensus reality that includes gravity and the rules of motion of mass and form no longer apply to us; most of us anyway. The Masters have their own possibilities, but for the majority of people who jump out of airplanes, the ground is freaking hard if you don't respect it. We have created evidence that mass exists and can cause harm to our physical form, and we believe it. The Masters, not so much. An empowered mind can learn the rules so they have something to bend. In a way, a skydiver is experiencing mastery in their own way. They step willingly into apparent risk and transform the probabilities into an unlikely bending of possibility, and forming it into a probable good time that others find impossible. We each live out our confirmation of our own beliefs, but when we notice how we are thinking and focusing, we can become more deliberate in creating the desired outcome. Without this level of awareness and mental discipline, we are slaves to our own solidified expectations.

I have noticed a fascinating phenomenon observing skydivers continuously for four decades. When I come across a skydiver who seems to have more fear than others, say, about a wild, spinning parachute malfunction, they will have a notably higher frequency of malfunctions. The live in the dream of what they fear, unconsciously gestating it, and then they will give birth to their dream. This most often is not deadly at all, just an inconvenience when driving all over the countryside looking for their lost main parachute. While it is not uncommon for some jumpers to rarely ever have a "cutaway", others, through worrying and half-expecting it, have them quite often.

Certainly, the effects of ones expectation of a negative experience is multifaceted. A nervous person may fall faster at pull-time, or experience instability during the opening process due to their stiff, awkward nature. This is not a person, but a state of mind. Most skydivers begin as the first category, and evolve into the second. They calm down, they learn how to fly, and they make the impossible happen.

The miracles that happen every single day in our skies are a demonstration of much more than the astounding technologies that we have developed in the name of joy.   It is the skydivers themselves who believe these miracles into being. They believe in the likelihood of brilliant skill and awareness and they focus their minds of the flow of making that happen, both physically and mentally. The malfunctions still show from time to time, even for the highly skilled skydivers, but there is no drama. It is just another version of fun, and we do what we have to at the time and we laugh about it at the campfire. Then we go to sleep and let it go, and in the morning, we choose again to visualize and create good parachute openings. We fill our minds with what we want. We continue to pack our canopies carefully, but not neurotically, because OCD is a real possibility in dangerous contexts. It is part of the territory.

If I do not check my equipment before putting it on, I am making a mistake. So, I do, and then I check it again before exiting the aircraft, because things may have shifted during the flight to jump altitude. If, on the other hand, I check my parachute 49 times on the way to altitude, I will make myself more nervous, or I risk dislodging something with my nervous fingers. It is that simple. Caution is rational and proportional, while fear is disproportionate and over-compensatory. Fear makes things more dangerous.

The distillation of infinite possibilities into the flight you write in your logbook is seen and created through the lens of your mind. The more you pave the way to one version of the experience, the more likely that reality is what you will experience. In harmony with this principle, I have observed that if you decide before you fly that you are a survivor, you will be. The same is true and in every moment of your life. The quantum field always says yes to our requests, and if we have a repeating loop of inadequacy, of a lack of cooperation with others, and ultimate disaster, it shows up with a perfect mirroring of our expectations. Thus, I urge all beings inhabiting 3D form: take heed of your mind. It speaks louder than you know.

## Keeping your Nose Up

When we fly, we must find a way to keep our eyes on the horizon, lest our downward gaze cause the aircraft to go to the depths of where we look. Life is dangerous for the fearfully fixated. We have all learned this through experience. A bad attitude is followed shortly by bad experiences that could have been avoided with a different mindset. This is why we must choose to nurture an uplifting perspective. Nobody is going to do it for you, and nothing works without it.

It is true that some have come to help you out. They are the healers and the teachers who point your mind toward the truth of your wellbeing. Nevertheless, these well-meaning souls must not become crutches to which you cling. Embrace the assistance and be thankful, but hold equally fast to your faith in yourself as the primary means to your own salvation. Nobody has your best interest at heart more than you.

Just as our loved ones warmly nurture us in times of trouble, we must learn how to play this role for ourselves within our own minds. Humans are not perfect, and we will have plenty of reasons to forgive ourselves for errors in judgment and failure in execution. Your worthiness still rings true despite your human imperfections, and the false beliefs into which we have all been indoctrinated. Your continuing intention to do well in your life, and to do good in the world, is your redeeming quality at all times. Despite human fear and folly, it is our best intentions that move us to inspired action, because that is who we really are. We must remember.

As we clarify our perceptions through lucid thinking, we see aspects of our reality that we believe need to change. We want some of these things to change so badly that we withhold our happiness until we get what we want. The catch is, things don't improve for us while we are still miserable. You simply can't get there for here. We lack access to our insightful, creative mindset when we are in the paradigm of suffering and victimhood. It is generally not the pain itself that causes our deepest suffering, but our interpretation of our experience. You can lament the inescapable reality, or you can accept and embrace its positive aspects. The world does not always serve the needy, but it always serves the thankful. Improvement begins with a perspective of gracious appreciation for the life we are living exactly as it is, and the people who are on this journey with us. We can celebrate the little things as gloriously as the big things. It is all a miracle. There is constructive value in everything, including that which we might judge as suffering.

Physical pain is a necessary component to inhabiting a human body. It can really hurt down here. This is not right or wrong, it just is. It is the "pain of pain" that causes the experience of deep suffering, and is brought forth through the comparisons of our present experience to the life we once had. It is through the clinging to the past that we create our ultimate torment. The transcendence of this mindset is always available to us when we surrender to radical acceptance of the here and now. The past is gone, and the future is just hope and fear, formless and irrelevant to our now moment. If we are to lift your spirits above all of the traps of the suffering mind, we must drift gently back into acceptance and appreciation for the value of our experience, exactly as it is. This is the power of transcendence called grace. We don't go around the suffering; we go through it with a lighter mind.

**Compassion Activation**

Someone somewhere is hurting. Someone is confused and scared. Someone is crying in pain. Someone is wallowing in devastating loss. What does your love make you want to do? Their experience can bring you down, or you can bring them up. When you learn how to keep your chin up and into the wind, you can teach others to fly too. The enlightening perspective is deeply contagious, because it is our natural state of being. As you feel into your sense of compassion, you can, if you dare, expand this tender feeling inward, because you are also part of the world that you wish to heal. In the process of loving others, without attachment to the outcome of our loving, we learn what being love is all about.

## The Way of Grace

The emotionally provocative, complex human experience is not sustainably controlled by brute force as the ego-mind would have it, but through the gentle influence of a nurturing guide. We influence our reality most powerfully with the finesse of charm, the glide of intelligent physics, and politeness of spirit. Grace moves mountains that aggression cannot even look upon.

Grace is the path through risk that floats above the danger because of the thoughts generated by a constructive mood of positive expectation. When we get into the swing of accepting and enjoying the flow, all risk softens, and safety becomes our reality. When we are in the peaceful mindset of the graceful way, we see the path of safety through the danger because our minds are congruent with the way of harmony.

## Wellbeing

What does it mean to be well? Truly feeling good to the core is a sense that few obtain and even fewer sustain, and it requires addressing many aspects of our being. Wellbeing is a holistic composite of all the aspects of you. It requires wellness of your body, your mind, and your spirit, the non-physical energy underlying all of it.

The physical body is a construct of the mind, however it is also comprised by the food we eat, the air we breathe, and many other aspects of our physical reality. What we consume becomes our new self in many ways, and if we eat lively foods that invigorate our form, we will feel better. Comfort food has little to do with our physical wellbeing, it is just an act of rebellion to fill a void. Wonder to yourself if your cravings are for the nutrification of your body, or merely a hunger for getting what you are owed by a world not terribly concerned with your needs. We all have binged a pint of ice cream because we believed we deserved it. We thought it would make us feel better, and maybe in that moment it did. Then comes the realization of what we actually ate, and the feeling of what it does to the body. Food is not for entertainment or emotional gratification, it is for minerals and vitamins, for protein and carbohydrates.

Ultimately, our bodies crave light. Our cells need the components to repair and utilize for living functions, and the sources of these components are readily available in the natural foods that are nurtured by the sun. In essence, plants are the will of the sunlight, as are you. If you stay away from processed foods full of chemicals to make them addictive and shelf-stable, and focus on what the body actually needs to thrive, you will feel the difference. You will be proud of your choices, and your mind will allow the absorption of these essential components.

The state of mind that we hold as we are eating is as significant as the content of our meals. If you gulp and chug and devour without a thought beyond how hungry you are, you are missing an essential step. You must feel thankful. You must be in awe and gratitude for all that had brought this food to your lips, and in holding this high vibration, your body is prepared to process what is eaten. Blessing the food, in the guidance I have received and the feeling I have experienced, make the food we eat bioavailable. It places us in the receiving mode of the energy, and it matters.

Even more important than food is the water that we drink. It must be clean and pure and without the human made chemicals that some once believed were necessary for clean pipes and healthy teeth. Above the contents of the water is the vibration assigned to it by the mind observing it. Your intention is imprinted within the structure of the water, and it remembers. Place your palm over your water glass and bless your water, and feel thankful. Awaken and invigorate the water with your intention, and it too will offer more goodness than it would have otherwise.

Exercise is no different. If you run just to get a tight ass, but you don't love running, you are missing the point. Enjoy your exercise, and enjoy how you feel about yourself as you walk, run dance and swim. Move gracefully and in a way that is kind to your body. Aggression is destructive and dangerous to the body, so make your efforts full of the grace that you are. Remember that exercise is a dish best served with a joy, because your likelihood of injury and overworking your muscles drops dramatically when you hold love in the process. It is a dance that allows your spirit to fully inhabit your form, and gives your body clear signals about what you would like to do more of in the future. Each motion is a pattern that the body remembers.

Ultimately what most needs healing and nurturing is the mind. We have been subjected to profoundly unloving ideas about the world and about ourselves. If we continue to navigate the world using this old software, we will have a bumpy ride indeed. The unloving mind, the ungracious mind, can only see and produce more of itself. This perspective sees the body as the enemy, as it rarely cooperates with our intentions when we are expecting nothing else. In order to transcend the basic software of the western mind, we must learn to love ourselves. In order to love ourselves, we must examine what we are not. We must unearth all the unloving thoughts in our minds, and let them go.

As we ask and answer the many hard questions, we find our spirits soaring, because in our conscious inquiry, we realize our truth. Likewise, we can uncover the resistance that we have been holding in our unconscious beliefs about ourselves, and about the world. Our mindset is implicitly based on these unconscious beliefs, and despite our certainty in their veracity, many of these unexamined core beliefs are untrue when examined in the light of day. We must explore our unloving beliefs with the most scrutiny, because they are the least true, and the most toxic to our wellbeing. Purge that which is unloving and therefore untrue, and meditate upon who you are in your brightest form. All aspects of wellbeing spring forth from the truth of you divinity and the power of your inspired mind.

## Forgiveness is a Doorway

It is time to cease the battling amongst ourselves. It has gotten way too nasty out there, and we need to stop. Regrettably, some still choose to cling tightly to their sledgehammers of judgment, a mindset devoid of grace and the fortitude of love's guidance. Life is hard in this realm, and in this mindset we want to bring the whole world down into our battles. Misery creates the darkness. This is the mindset of the poo-slinging righteous warriors who have not yet had a long overdue attitude adjustment.

When we are immersed in this mindset, we are blindfolded in the playing out of a strict and unkind role, and are fighting in terror against the dying of the light that we fear will go out. We see others as separate and at times much less valuable than ourselves. Those in judgment always find enemies, the people who we have snap-judged on the shoddiest of evidence clouded with incorrect information skewed by negative expectation. We don't know as much as we think. The mind in separation must deem itself infallible because it is terrified of being found mentally inept. In this polarity, we humans sometimes find ourselves playing the role of the bully, using the force of our loud voice and strongly worded weapons of logic.

The bully only pretends to be brave, by being territorially aggressive in its displays. Through the ego's defensiveness and faith in attack as a means to its safety, it foments its own self destruction by losing its connection to the energy of love. When a person chooses to close their heart, love can't get in.

We all have our moments that need forgiving, things we have said and done that we intend to do quite differently next time around. We all fall down from our original blueprint of lovingkindness. Some, while they're down there, have a habit of grabbing the nearest pig shit and try to shove it into the mouths of "the morons": ghosts they swat at, old patterns projected onto new people, and the shit-shit goes on. It is thusly wise to keep one's head down at times when poo is flying through the air. If you stand up on one side or the other, you get covered in poo. That is the nature of a shitshow, and this, my good people, is what we are in. The only ones who end up smelling good are those bold enough to see the beauty in all situations and in all people. It takes gonads, metaphorically speaking, to really walk that walk, but real people do it every day.

Vast and wide is the courage required for authentic, persistent forgiveness. For there are thousands of situations that trigger our ego consciousness of enmity and our selfish servitude to fear. We must awaken to and forgive each of them, one at a time. Through a commitment to love all beings always, we alchemize our repulsions and fears, and despite the painful process of letting go of our judgments, we become free to be the kindest, happiest versions of ourselves. Each in our own way, we will reach out toward forgiveness, so that we ourselves can live in the lightness of joy, our shared goal of living in peaceful bliss. We must forgive to live.

These people that we were so angry with are our teammates in life, part of our whole being. They are our families, our neighbors, our coworkers, people with whom we once felt true friendships. These bonds can be rekindled if we try. It was always the low hanging fruit of true value to the soul. The soul craves upliftment, but first we must shed our excess load. For the aircraft to fly, some things just can't go in the suitcase, like the lead bars of judgment that make us much less kind and understanding than we could be. We must seek to understand and appreciate. We must learn about others' perspectives, even though much of the time, we choose to be like us and not like them. So what? Let others be.

Our way forward is an emotional journey. It is a journey into honesty in how we see our world and how we believe things to be. We must look again at the judgments we were taught to enforce without the regret of causing harm. We must become gracefully uncertain enough to put down our sledgehammer of righteousness. It is in the releasing of the servitude to certainty that we become open.

When a mind wanders and wonders its way into alternatives, it considers the new possibilities. The mind solves needs and provides for our wants as well, provided that we are patient and diligent in our creative process. As we learn the lessons of life and the wisdom of love, our realizations may offer a challenging path that the soul thrives, having lived this experience. Do not be so quick to judge what is right for another when the evidence of their wider being is greater than we know. They mean something to someone who loves them, even when they are acting like an ass-hat.

Forgive, but do not stand in the campfire. In this fire, humanity's soul is purified of past judgments and old battles that have waged for longer than we can remember. The places and names have changed throughout history, but the urge to attack is what must be addressed. Fear and hate cannot be destroyed, only alchemized, and left to die on the vine. It is a fruit we have found sour, and we can apply our gained wisdom to not eat it again. If we release and purge in a ritualized, deliberate act of letting go, these old ways, unfueled, will be forgotten.

You may choose to write it all out on paper and then burn it. When you become clear about what you think you are pissed about, you can examine the validity of our thinking through our original intention of harmony and peace. See how these judgments were not of your own making. The origin is the worthless teaching of a civilization that has strayed from kindness and caring for others, based in the illusion of separation.

We can and we must and we will.  We will get this human cooperation thing dialed in through each of us doing the work. It is called a Forgiveness Practice, and it is the only way out of the insanity of what the human world has been in order to be such putzes to each other and the rest of the species on the planet. Let's get it together people, there's work to be done.

Forgive them, for they have forgotten that they desire love above all else. Forgive yourself for the same amnesia.

## Transcending Panic

Love is not accessible from a state of panic, and neither is skill. Fear is a construct of the ego mind, the separated mindset that cannot experience love in its true form. The ego identifies with the frail body, and the feeling of lack. Love is abundance in all its forms, and stems from a mindset independent from the ego mind. The ego is based in fear, lack and isolation. The ego is so sure of its judgments that it cannot conceive of anything else.

Relax into the grace of uncertainty. Panic is brought to a head due through our judgments, drawing a negative conclusion and looping it in our minds through our choice to cause harm in our mind. You don't know for sure that you are going to die, or that someone you love will leave you. You do not know that you are going to run out of money and starve to death, all alone, in abject shame. These are the kinds of thoughts that lead to panic and then apathy, the freezing of the mind fixated on the most revolting possibilities. Fear attracts us to what we strive to repel, because we create the content of our minds in the physical world. If you are in panic, you are not in your right mind. You are in the lower compartment of consciousness when you are afraid, but even in such places, you can remember that there is another feeling that can be conjured. You can visualize what the present situation causes you to desire. Your mind, your choice.

## Wholistic Discernment

Begin with the inquiry: "Is this true?" Awaken to your assumptions, your expectations based on the past. Next ask yourself: "Does this thought expand my realm or contract it?" Fear closes doors and locks them tight, costing us the evolution of our consciousness through the brave pursuit of creative expansion. Then ask: "Is it connecting?" The purpose of our existence is to expand the complexity and harmony of our mutual collaborations, and fear has a way of stopping such things in their tracks. If a risk is based in love, the fear becomes irrelevant, and will dissolve as you focus on compassion-driven action. You will have the wind at your back, because this benevolent Universe supports love in all its forms. If the emotion is merely a construct of the insecure fear-based mindset, stop and consider exactly *HOW* you can proceed with caution, despite your fear. You may have to meditate and clarify your mind first, but these harrowing roads are the ones that lead to our ultimate victories of virtue and meaning, the alchemy of fear into love.

Everything is an adventure, subject to necessary adaptations and emotional redirection. If you thought the past was challenging, wait until you get a load of the future. You better be on your toes. This is going to be the craziest set of back-to-back stunts ever performed, and the tests will be physical, intellectual, emotional and spiritual. You are going hear yourself say: *"I have to do what?"*, in shock of the necessary path ahead. I said that often when my children were young, especially when changing diapers. That is life on earth. We expand through surprise challenges that show us who we can be when we have to, and we choose to expand into being our best self. Are you ready to step into the light of who you really are?

## The Inspiring Nature of the Adventuresome Mind

The feeling of grounded, mental balance lies at the core of wellbeing. Mental balance feels serene within the dynamic pursuits of life's rollercoaster ride through physical reality. As we follow up on our ongoing, ever-evolving intentions, we become happier and more effective in life. This feeling begs us forward into challenge, to demonstrate the power of awareness in the quest for graceful skill in motion. It is the passionate exploration of meaningful risk that makes life work, and makes life worth living. Even within the unfolding of our life's purpose, we must re-center ourselves and reconnect, again and again, with the point of focus that is our intention.

Each flight, each feat of imaginative, creative heroism is a choice to demonstrate the magic of positive expectation in the manifestation of our intention. Fearless optimism is at the root of all constructive creativity, and every heart-driven jaunt into meaningful danger. We succeed because we believe. Blessed are those who pursue their passion with fearless commitment.

"Shall we risk it for a biscuit?" my teammate and fellow test pilot Tony Uragallo used to say. If the value of success is high and the hazard is worth taking, we must take risks if we are to be more than just a mundane citizen playing it safe. Our true nature requires us to take on *reasonable* challenges, and chance failure to have the possibility of worthwhile gains. This is not just what we do, it is who we are.

On the other hand, we must not be stupid. Risk is dangerous. If the feeling in your gut says no, do not proceed. It may not be an absolute "No", but simply a "Not Just Yet". My friend Tina Louise Spaulding often says: "If it's not a Hell Yes, it's a no." Our guidance comes in many forms, and if we are to be creative thought-leaders, we must begin with trusting our inner voice. Regardless of what others are doing and saying, if you cannot trust your gut, you are in the clouds with no instruments.

Some of our emotional experiences are based in programmed responses, learning from others and from our own life story. Other times our sensations of avoidance and attraction are based on the wise council of the Higher Mind within. We can discern the source of our guidance by how it makes us feel. If it feels like fear, fury or judgmental repulsion, it is worth re-examining. These lower emotions are the gatekeepers of the insecure ego mind, the voice of the physical body desperately trying to stay alive. The ego does not consult compassion, as it is deeply selfish in its though system, alone and in danger, the ego thrashes and claws its way to the top without a care of the damage it causes, or the feelings it hurts.

Ego is the mind separated from Source. It is a mindset based in lack, fear, lust and hate. It is the mind lost in the funhouse of 3D, confused about what is true, not understanding that what is seen in the many mirrors is all a projection of mind. Only love is the true self.

The ego within us all is insane. It is fearful. It is hateful and jealous and will destroy and kill to stay alive. It is the voice of the body, tasked with keeping you alive. It will never go away completely, but if we love it as it is, and step out of its thought system, we can expand our consciousness to the love that we really are.

Sit in silence, out in the sunshine, and let it all go. Let go of the assumptions and judgments, and the urge to attack and defend. Make peace within your mind, and realize the harmony of the world. Cease the struggle that the ego mind craves, and expand into the larger consciousness that you are, the spark of loving consciousness that is the basis of all of us. We are more than our separated minds, and if we dare, we can be at peace.


## Facing Your Dragon

Have you released your deepest pain, the heart of your suffering as a human being? What happened that you gave permission to break you? It did not break you. You are still here, fighting the good fight between love and fear, awakening to your impressive existence. The only reason these things echo in our minds is because we choose with the free will of our sovereign minds to choose something other than a loving perspective. You're not nothing, and to your parents and the Parent of all of us, you are perfect and beautiful and valued beyond measure.

Forgiveness and recreation come through rituals of spoken words, written words, and brave compassionate deeds. In our acts of kind mercy, humanity demonstrates its ability to forgive the past. Through the release of the burden of unloving lies, we root out and release the untruth from within us. In becoming more congruent with the grace-filled truths we become lighter, softer, and more at ease. Grace is not only yielding but is also the fire of creation in the awakening to the power of an inspired mind who allows itself to wonder. It is through our faith that allows belief in our dreams, and with determined attention, become our reality. In doing so, we show our unique properties of light, just being ourselves.

When a mind awakens unto itself, it expands its focus to a larger frame of reference, and more is possible. The human imagination is boundless in the truest sense of the word. If we let our minds wonder what our lives were like if things were perfect, what do we see. Each of us has a unique dream, and our dreams are expanding as we become more aware of what we prefer. We dip into an experience that is the opposite of what we prefer, and we awaken a truth that presents a larger vision of what could be.

State these dreams aloud, with your voice. Realize your truth, accept who you are, and embrace it with all of your being. It starts with the moment of realization that you have the intention to live an inspired life, a path of virtue. You have always intended to be a good human being, your way. Remember that. Rekindle the vision called you. Say your full name. Speak it proudly. Claim the space of your full being, all of you, awakened in this shining moment.

Draw a deep breath into your lungs right now, ever so deep, hold for the same amount of time it took to inhale, and let yourself relax into the relief of remembering that you are a genuinely well-intended person. Slowly release your breath in this moment of visceral knowing of who you are. Meaning well isn't everything, but it certainly is more than enough to go the distance. With all of life's ups and downs, all we really have at the end of the day is our unwavering desire for unilateral improvement in our lives, and in the world around us. Remember your essence, and you will realize that you are a force of nature.

**Intend Powerfully**

All improvement begins with intention.

How can you become a better version of you? The answer is clarified intention, backed up with the heroic fortitude of follow-through.

Do you intend to be physically healthy? What are you doing about it? Do you intend to be strong and flexible? What actions are you taking to make this so? Do you intend to have stamina and enthusiasm? How do you bring empowering energy into your mind? Do you seek inspired purpose? Are you complaining or are you envisioning the alternative to what you despise about your life. Do you intend to smile authentically? Do you ponder thoughts of gratitude, and celebrate your life in moments of profound silence? Do you intend to be a fun person? Will you let yourself laugh?

Do you intend to enjoy the exciting ride of being in physical form? Do you choose to have incorrigible enthusiasm for your life, exactly as it is, on your way to better?

Do you silence your mind so that you can remember your true essence? Will you a linger a little longer in the stillness at the top of your breath, and again at the bottom, in mergence with cosmic consciousness?

Do you intend to use your happiness and balance to help others find happiness and balance? Do you value the path of service to others? How might your ways of helping others uplift your vibration and your light? As a spiritual being having a physical experience, do you remember that this endeavor is/was voluntary?

Here's the thing. Awakening has to happen every single day, like taking yet another shower, another meal, watching another sunrise. You will get up again tomorrow and you will not be fully awake. You will inhabit the aspect of your personality that reboots to the version that has forgotten your connection. State it again, every day:

I am connected to the feeling of love and joy in this moment.

I am inspired by life and delighted to live it.

I am grateful for all that transpires, the easy lessons as well as the more challenging ones. I revel in the expansion of my knowing.

I am glad for the realization that bliss is always a breath away, the knowing of Oneness is the highest vibration that I am.

Choose to begin your day consciously each morning, with rituals of grace-filled statements, and speak your clear intention to the Universe. It does come back again and again, but often some life drama will send us into its loop of roles and thoughts that spring forth like clockworks, seemingly causing our actions as if we are on autopilot. Depending on where we are with respect to the joyful loving emotions, we may be in for yet another wild ride.

Human experience is governed more by emotion than all other factors combined. If I teach someone how to operate a parachute, the emotional journey is ultimately what determines the outcome of their jump. There are undoubtedly other factors at work, but in the end, the way we react to our world is of pivotal importance. We must therefore make our emotional awareness a focus of every undertaking, in all moments. If we explore the belief structures that underly our emotions, we can uncover many negative beliefs that we no longer wish to hold in our minds as true.

**Risk is Subjective**

Danger can be done safely. Some risks are insurmountable in some moments, but when the green light comes on, the inspired adventurer clears their own path with their solution-oriented state of mind. If we find a stunt worth taking, a demonstrated skill amidst risk, we can skew the odds in our favor with our mindset. We become supremely competent and insightful due to our buoyant attitude. This feeling can be transferred into other areas of our lives, into whatever matters most right now. All of us have access to this feeling.

The confidence that we foster through the transcendence of barriers makes us larger. As we become more, we have the choice of milking the feeling for our own benefit, or extending the feeling to someone who needs it. There is always someone in need. They need your love and your insights, because all they can feel is their pain. Your patience will be necessary, as will your ability to cheer yourself up again after playing the role of the uplifter. After helping lift someone up, sometimes we feel a drop in our vibration. The assisting of others is not without its dangers, and it is nearly inevitable that your happiness level will sometimes fall as a result of working with people in a challenging mindset. It's like clapping the erasers after school is over. Clear those chakras.

Those you try to help will sometimes take your assistance, your heart-felt inspiring words and actions. Other times will be more trying, and will require you to hold a clear picture in your mind of something that is not here yet. All improvements begin first in the mind, and then life challenges our vision. The evidence does not point upward right away. Patience and imagination is necessary for healing and improving circumstances that have fallen into the chaos of the unloving mindset. In some cases, they are not ready to change their perspective. "Not-giving up on them" can either lead you to break yourself trying, or a loving acceptance of their journey, as it is. Transcend your fixation on the outcome, and simply enjoy the experience of shining light.

## Emotional Stabilization

I have noticed that the longer I am afraid, the longer it takes for me to calm down. The longer I am angry, the longer it takes for me to cheer up. On the flip side of the coin called "emotional inertia", the longer I am happy, the harder it is to make me miserable. When I am happy, you just can't bug me. I find the most constructive way to interpret the world around me is to trust that all is well, or leading to better. I may still rendezvous with trouble for the benefit of my learning, but in the end my positive expectation leads me in the general direction of up.

When I deliberately ponder my thoughts upward toward a better feeling, I open the door for more: more happiness, more success, more enjoyment in life. Good leads to better just as bad leads to worse. That is the tendency of the inertia, but not the destiny of the person who decides to be the pilot of their emotions, and thus consciously navigate their life experience.

## The Irrationality of Trepidation

Fear causes the mind to investigate reasons to be afraid, not reasons to be relieved. It is a disproportionate weighting of the unlikely possibility that you are screwed. Rationality is logical math, and fear will have no part in it. Be the sentience behind the thoughts, and notice the high probability that everything is going to be alright.

Force often disguises itself as power, but it is an ill-conceived, half-baked expression of true power, and its reign is always short-lived. Love is always present in true power, because moral influence always includes compassion. When we are in fear, we are without love. Fear causes us to think selfishly and shortsightedly, and has little care for the experiences of others. When we bash through the world with aggression, we are lost in fear and fury, and the side effects of our ungraceful way is resistance. Love has no resistance. It is the graceful path that leads to cooperation and a flow of life that sustains wellbeing. Grace is an aspect of love, and we all know that love is The Way.

There is great wisdom in emotion. When we feel negatively, it is an indication that it is time to let up on the gas pedal and rethink where we are going with our thoughts,. Speed only feels good when it is coupled with well-conceived intention and joy.

Speeding up when our gut is telling us to slow down is often the last thing we do before feeling profound regret. The mind that hungers to win ignores its inner guidance. We grew up in a world that rewards physical power and forceful means, and so we have been trained into ignoring the soft, small voice of kindness and grace. Ego screams, love whispers. Silence your mind, especially in moments of heat and speed, and listen for your loving guidance from within.

The Wisdom is Within.


## On the Topic of Grief

As a human being, I know that you have suffered in the pain of loss. There are many people in your life that you love and miss. You can feel the missing piece of yourself, or you can experience your love for them in this moment. You can remember their presence, their personality, their countenance, and they are here in your mind, alive and well. The people that you love who are not with you are coming back, in one form or another, because you love each other. Your souls are part of a family, demonstrated through understanding and forgiveness, because it is loving to be kind. You know what your physically displaced loved one would say in this moment. What would their loving perspective say to you in this moment? What would their belief in you cause them to say? This is the legacy of their love that lives on in you. It never dies, and thankfully, neither does anybody in any meaningful sense of the word. The container of the body falls away because it lives in the impermanent plane of existence called 3D Planet Earth. There are rules here, and even if you realize that you are in infinite being, even if you know that your mind and God's Mind can be One, your body will fall away, because that is what happens here. We all agreed to this, we accept it, and we move on.

We will still exist in our awareness of a different experience. We have all been there, it's where we came from and where we are going. We choose to forget over on this side, it's part of the plan. When you squeeze your infinite nature into a human body, it's a really tight squeeze, and we leave our expanded consciousness at the door. We forget.

Then, noticing the details of our experience, we see cracks in the foundation. We explore truth, in our own way, and we figure out that there is more going on here than meets the eye. These other characters are of the same Mind, because there is one being with many faces, connected in a web of the Akashic field, the history of the universe. In this book of records is the story of the love that we've made in our various experiences, the high-water marks of our soul's journey. In this experience of knowing all that you are there is no grief. Then we let go of knowing our connection through a choice to explore separation, and we are sent on a self-assigned journey of creation. Our soul has many parts, a web of lights in the darkness, your soul family. We choose to continue to intermingle, because we care so much about each other's evolution toward knowing what is means to be human. We help remind each other to find our connection to our inner being. We are both parent and child, fiend and friend, the hated one and loved one. We play these roles for each other as a magnificent gift, orchestrating a balance of opposites, coming to know love through that drama. It is a play that we remake again and again, with many of our loved cast members, and inevitably and excitingly, brand new souls with whom you have not yet interacted.  That would be supremely terrifying if we all weren't ultimately on the same team.

Your team is here, and it always WILL BE.

Those beings who you loved so much, the ones you call the "Dearly Departed", the ones you have cried for in anguish of their death, they have not departed, you did. You stopped talking to them and wondering what they would say. You stopped remembering their smile and their warm embrace. You left them, but there are right here. They are an image right before you, a dreamscape experience that is absolutely real to you in this moment, if you can surrender to the imagination that God gave you. In this remembrance of this specific love, expand and extend this feeling of connection outward to all who suffer in loss. Let them feel the explosion of light that springs forth in your realization of your connection.

## The Upliftment of the World

To uplift others with one's connection through love, one must continue to nurture the vibration within oneself. If you still hold pain in your heart for someone that you consider lost to you, do yourself a profound favor and accept and release that mindset. Find a way to touch it, love it and let go of it. You have a life to live, and you need your full attention to be present so you can do what you came here to do. Holding on to sadness and pain is a choice based on a limited perspective, one that has chosen separation and time and physical matter as being all that is. Many believe in the perspective that only what we can see with our eyes is real, and yet we know of that vast domains of the full spectrum of light are invisible to the human eye. Accept that the mind of your beloved is here, however your mind needs to frame the new version of your relationship. When you feel your connection, you can let go of your attachment and move ahead to focus your full attention on the pursuit of the passion in your life. The emotional weight is over your baggage allowance in your lighter form, so you must leave it behind. You never leave your beloved behind; it is your belief in a loss that requires further mourning which will drift over the horizon. This will allow you to become a larger container for love, and more of you will be available to invest in your present moment.

The more love-filled version of you is absolutely here and now and full-on stoked. Any other version of you has some shadow-purging to take on. Face your demons and your anguish: see it, feel it, touch it, taste it to know what it is. Lies are conjured by the ego mind to keep you small and humble because the ego believes this is necessary for your safety. Understand the perspective, and then pivot toward the larger point of view. Let the suffering go, again as it arises, as long as you both shall live.

*

It is profoundly loving to treat others with the love you only wish you could allow yourself to deserve. You can hope for your worthiness of this level of love, or you can earn it. Love harder. Love in more ways. Love now.

Platitudes are the finger pointing to the moon, helpful and kind, however one must take the leap into feeling it. Let the feeling of loving joy flow over your entire being right now this very moment. Let it inhabit your form and move you in the cosmic dance of wellbeing in motion. Move in your way, in the flow that feels best to you. Let this exquisite feeling of grace carry you into wherever feels right. Joy is motion. Joy is harmony. Joy is playful and creative and fun. This is the essence of the Divine, including You. Feel the emotional sensation of love, and you will know that you are home.

*

## On the Topic of Nature

The Garden is glad you are here, and you are welcome.

Tread lovingly, knowing that the Garden loves you back. Nature is your Mother, and she will do whatever She can to keep Life afloat. Ignore Her or subject Her to generations of disrespect, and She can shake us off like a horse dispatching a bothersome fly from its back.

Thank your Mother. Love your Mother. Respect your Mother. She is the only home we've got. More than a home, the Being Called Gaia is not just a planet we live upon, it is you. There is no separation between the beings that comprise a body and the body as a whole. When you look upon the beauty of the earth, of the living balance of unimaginable complexity, know that you are in awe of yourself. When Gaia looks upon the component cells of Her being and feels our gratitude and knows our kindness, she offers her glad tidings in the form of the cornucopia that sustains our existence. Nature is the unfolding of the will to live, having sprung forth from the same love that created you. The Mother and the Father are One, different perspectives on the Love That is All.

This Earth is a Miracle, and so are we.

It is time to heal the soil and build a garden that gives both to the people and to the earth. Purge the toxins out of the soil with ash and charcoal, and put those worms to work in your worm farm. They know how to make the best soil imaginable. Give them a chance to save us all. Give the bees something to pollinate, and humanity the nutrient-dense food we deserve.

Plant your seeds now, because we're going to need really good food. Watch the seedling grow, proud creator, and feel calmed by the thriving life in your garden. Regenerate the soil and make it fruitful, and be healed in the process.

Shed your aversion to getting dirty, and feel the soil of earth under your bare feet. Feel the warm grass between your toes, and the sunshine on your face. This is the home of the human being, frolicking in the Garden, as intended.

Life force energy is a real thing. Go getcha some.

*

**Nature Wisdom**

The forests and seas are our touchstone. When we observe the ways of the natural world, we realize how this wisdom may provide guidance for our own lives. The ways of mother earth are brilliant and complex and simple and perfect. There is no excess or shortage that is not immediately recognized and addressed with an appropriate adaptation. Nature is willing to change. It is not limited by the cobwebs of fear the way humanity has experienced. Nature is aware of itself, and always know where the sun and the moon are, the seasons and the needs that keep each species in balance with itself and with the other species in which its existence is inseparably intertwined.

We are no different. Our lives become out of balance, first will a little tip to the left as it a were, a little skid in the turn, and then we get stronger and stronger wisdom and guidance to do things differently moving forward. The trick is, we must always be on the lookout for wisdom. It shows up in the most unexpected places, often through the most unexpected people of any age. As each tree has its own inner knowing where the light is, where the roots can grow, when to brace for challenge and when it time to thrive and expand beyond expectation.

Humans do not always do things in harmony with nature, which is why we need to go back to school one might say, under the tall classroom of the wooded lands of the earth. We must watch water flow and plants sway in the breeze. We must honor the experiences of each life form and point of existence such as a rock or fallen tree, each with its own view and slowly flowing motion toward entropy and return to the cycles of the living earth. These processes give us life.

If one were to consider being a scuba diver, learning about the airflow system that keeps you from coming back to the surface, you would listen and learn and ask lots of good questions. Your desire to have a gracefully flowing experience without hard learning moments is what grabs your attention. The soil that grows your food, the sky that fills your lungs, all of these things are gifts of a generous mother who is about at her wits end. We moved out of her house and now we are the noisy neighbor with several eviction noticed taped to the front door. How many signs do we need to turn our ways around? It is time, right now, to take the ecosystem more seriously. This begins with meeting her on her own ground, not on our turf.

Connecting with nature is essential to remember our oneness with her being. We are like cells of her complex body, so helping, some conflicting with the balance that she needs. When we sit and deeply inhale and ponder her, we become part of her. In truth, we were always part of her body, we have just pretended we are living on her, separate and independent. Mama's still cooking your dinner, and we need to thank her more often.

Think of it as a visit to Grandma's House, where you always feel so welcome and you always have a much better time than you expected. Envision in your mind how a loving grandparent feels about their grandchild. This is how nature feels about you, and hugging a tree or applauding a sunset is how you return the favor. Paying the living ecosystem back is a two way street, with benefits all around. You get exercise, good things to breath into your lungs that the trees produce that make you physically healthier. The studied go on and on, supporting robust evidence that being in nature makes a dramatic difference in many dimensions of human wellbeing.

Just being in the forest does seem to reduce blood pressure as effectively as non-natural medications. Breathing the aroma of many pine trees, in particular, clearly shows reduced physical inflammation, which is correlated with most illness. All these tangible benefits aside, meditating in a quiet, natural setting is true bliss. What would this world be like if everyone experienced pure bliss in nature on a daily, or even just weekly basis? Imagine. Wonder. Do your time in the woods, and many are going to do the same.

Getting out into nature is the logical next step for getting to the end of the internet. Yes, it keeps growing, however there is a certain moment in our experience in which we have just had enough salty and we crave something sweet. This is why the phones are being turned off and life is switching on for so many. We hunger for direct experience, sensations and novelty, amazement and wonder. All this can be yours for the low cost of not-a-dime.

When you go out, do some prep time in visualizing what you might wish you had with you, and what you were going to bring but will just weight in your backpack. Many of the things we cling to in life are liabilities and not actually assets. They are just what we believe at the time we couldn't do without, and we choose to change our minds about the packing list, the friends list, and the to do lists of our lives. The metaphorical patterns from our adventures in nature parallel our lives so closely because we are part of the same physics of the world. We are within nature, and we are subject to her ways, but we have not learned them.

The old ways were passed down, the ways of living in harmony of the earth, but now they are forgotten and lost on so many. As nature knocks more and more loudly on our doors, we all eventually look up phone our phones and computers and take of our VR headsets and sit in a field and smile. Eventually all crave the peace and grace of the magnificent beauty of the living beings that we live alongside on the surface of the greatest planet in the universe as far as I'm concerned, but I am biased, as a proud earthling. When we expand and join with the wind and water, plants and animals, we remember the meaning of the old ways, and we begin to envision new ways.

Harmony is about balance. It is about seeing the needs of all the other players, and reaching toward everyone getting what they need and where they want to go. What does that plant, that animal, that river want to do? What does it need to survive in its way and how can we help it get along its way? Mostly, humans need to just leave the natural processes alone to flourish without pollution and noise and disturbance of any kind. New chemicals may create something interesting for humans that the result of the ecosystem has no interest in whatsoever. Our needs end where her needs begin.

When we walk in nature, we see her. We watch her processes and we have no alternative but to feel awe and love and respect for the hardiness and resilience of living beings cleverly designed to keep being alive. The wings of a hummingbird, the tail of the whale, or the perfection of our hands to create and hold and hug. Pondering these things is a transcendent feeling of sublime connection to all that is. The unity of the earth is a most enlightening realization, including all of the creatures up to and including the noisy beautiful monkeys that smell like soap.

She knows you are here. She hears and smells and feels just like you, but her ears are much bigger and hear all that happens upon and within her. When one or more are gathers in praise of the earth and that which allowed it to come into being, we begin to see the intelligent inevitability of all that happens in this universe. The sun rises, the moon pulls the oceans, the trees bear their fruit and offer it to all because that is their nature. It is our nature to pick up track on the trail, and wrap our arms around a tree and linger in loving connection. We are here to hug the trees, and each other. The rest is just check boxes made up by people who want something from you. Want connection. Want awe.

Want vibrant elation in wonderment of the gliding whoosh of a flock of geese settling onto a still mountain pond. Your day, your choice. The good apple is always here for the picking.

Did you know that the creator of our home, and the home itself, loves us and wants us to continue being and asset to the world? The loving forgiveness is ever-present and always available, and what would make your grandma bubble over with pride is to see you spending more time in bliss within her garden. It makes her smile to see her children smile. Its what love does. We are given what we deserve, and we deserve the world, even though sometimes we are messy and shortsighted. She forgives us and hopes we will do the right thing. She hopes we clean up after ourselves and leave the place better than we found it. We have the know-how to replenish the soils, and now we can choose to muster the will.

When your desire to be of assistance to the earth is strong enough, you will take action. You will ask the right questions and you will begin your own family's composting system, complete with the worms that were literally designed to turn vegetative matter into organically diverse soil. The consequential nutritional benefits to the food you grow in your little garden will be divine. That helps her, and it helps you. Healthy clean soil and healthy clean food loads the medical system less, because you and your family are far more likely to experience robust health.

Improvement are required because what we used to do was much too messy and toxic. We have wonderful imaginations, and we can conjure the solutions to all the imbalances that we have created? How has your life impacted the flow of harmony, and added unnatural components to our ecosystem? How can you reduce this impact, and how will you feel when you do? When you walk amongst the living elemental components of our world with a deliberately expanded awareness, the insight about how we can be of service to her rise to the surface of our minds.

What does mother earth need from you? For starters, she asked me to tell you to quiet down, and listen to her many sounds. She wants you to calm your vibe, and send out a radiance of abundant love and desire for flowing coexistence with all in your realm. She wants you to see that you are part of her team. She wants you to stop fighting amongst yourselves and become peaceful like her. She wants you to put your worries to rest, so that you can see the priorities of life in a new way. She wants you to ponder wellbeing and celebrate existence. She wants you to be happy.

You can be happy in a speedboat. You can be happy on a noisy motorcycle. You can be happy ripping up the side of a mountain on a motorbike, digging into her soil and eroding her surfaces. It is your choice, and she allows it. She is glad to see you smile. She also experiences the natural consequences of the oil dripping from the engine and the exhaust your machines spew forth into her skies. Ponder the effects of your happiness. It can be derived from many places, and some have more natural consequences than others.

You can be happy planting a garden. You can be happy eating food off the vine. You can be happy washing the oil from sea birds as you return them to the sky. You can be happy making music in the forest, joining hands in a sacred dance. You can be happy all alone, with your bottom upon the land.

The meaning of your life is derived from the degree to which you take action on your moments of inspiration and perspective, when you realize what is right. You can look back, in this moment in your life of pivotal significance, and realize that the way were is now in the past for a reason. It is the past because you no longer desire it to be your present, otherwise it would still be so. The future is made in the now moment of your actions, words deeds and awakenings. Awakening to the truth of who you are, in your unique life, is a dish best served in the context of a natural environment, because that is what you are.

Trying for a profound insight in the connect of the human culture we have become reliant upon for our ideas has come up short. We ran out of meaning as our pursuits proved shallow and hollow and devoid of our true nature. Nature is creative and joyful and free. If a human feels down and without inspiration, it is because they have forgotten who they are. You are nature, and playing by any other rule book will lead to frustration.

Who's rulebook do you live by? Was it your parents who showed you how to be and what to want? Was it the school system that formed your goals for you, or the movies you watched? Cast aside the flaming hoops that the world has presented before you, and wonder what would be better than this. Wonder about the version of you that is no longer afraid of disappointing the expectations of others and focus your energy on your own vision for you, based in your highest inspiration.

An inspired mind spring forth by an inspired body, moving in natural unjudged ways in natural un-humanized environments. Tune your mind into the graceful ways of the natural world and you will realize that this is your nature in your innermost essence. It feels good because you are home, and you can feel it. You are many versions of yourself, some more energetic than others. Call forth all that you are when you are immersed in beautiful places, and connect to the larger you that includes all you can see, feel taste and touch.

When you look into the clouds above and you see a bird of prey riding thermal life in its effortless means to remain aloft, take his spirit as your own. Share his elevated view, and his freedom of spirit. Thank the bird for his gifts, and offer your joy in return. Your glee expands him, and his existence expands who and what you are. The bird is now a part of you, and you are forever, more.

When we observe nature from the inside, as a part of it all, we experience something transcendent. We experience divine connection, and we expand beyond the ego's thought system. We see that our feeling of separateness from the world was an illusion, and that lie was making us unhappy. You are part of this living world, and every bit as beautiful as the butterflies and graceful gazelles that spur your awe. When you enter the silence and observe the world, we become the world.

*"We sit together, the mountain and me,*

*until only the mountain remains."*

*-Li Po*

## Your Original Happiness

Happiness is always a possibility, because the grand design has always given us a way forward because we are all favored children of the Divine Universe, and a Parent always wants the children to be happy. The Creator is in love with the Creation, making joy the easiest and most natural emotion shared by all of humanity. We were all children once. We all remember that laughter was not just something that we did to entertain ourselves, it is part of our natural way of being. We are a chip of the 'Ole Block.

Happy grows as happy does. If you feel joyful, carry out whatever comes to mind. Following your bliss is a wide range of possible evolutions within your mind. Joy is creation in the present with an unfathomable flow of energy moving in that direction, toward that experience which brings joy to the world of mankind. So shines a bright light in the darkness of a weary world suffering in the separated mind.

Loves calls us forth out of the depths of our illusions of being apart from the mind of the One. The voice of love speaks the truth that you are always connected to God's Great Mind. I know that is a hugely loaded word, and different interpretations cause confusion of expectations about what is meant. In my understanding, God is the basis of your mind, my mind, and indeed all minds everywhere. Source Consciousness, that infinite Energy of Creation it is a collection of all the unity of all the beings everywhere. It has a beingness far vaster than can be perceived from anywhere in the physical matrix of three-dimensional matter.

Your human truth is poignant for you, but not all things matter to all beings. What matters most when we are on the other side, in our non-physical expanded consciousness, is the evolution of your soul in its intention to expand and grow and learn and live a sentient life experience in a human form. The lively spark of consciousness that you are is a thought in the mind of the All-That-Is, and you have access to more than you know. This is because there is one love shared throughout the universes, one mind, one tone, one light, one sensation of exuberant creativity and joyful expectation without resistance to the outcome. Source Mind is the urge of life, the cooperative creative energy some call love, some call Grace, and some call God, others Source, while others refer to this connected state of beingness as the Quantum Field.

It is time to have a direct conversation with that Mind.

The One awaits your allowance of your worthiness. The experience of connection with the Divine requires an energetic shift of vibration to the vicinity of the wider mind we reach to connect with. It is through the sensation of elation, thankful and joyful, that we have the realization of being back in the Garden once called Eden. It is within us always to open our eyes to see, and our ears to hear the Unified Voice of Love. When you ask for an audience with the Big Kahuna, it is always given.

The gates to the Garden are open.

## The Red Pill: The Truth of Oneness

We all return home, and from the ultimate truth, we never left. The illusion is powerfully convincing, with the enduring nature of suffering on this planet. It helps to remember that nothing we see here has any bearing on the truth of what is. We never left the loving arms of the Divine Parent. It's a pretty intense dream though, and it seems to be taking forever. Look within, beyond the physical shell that the ego has created all around it to feel separate and independent. Look deeper inside, to the I AM under it all. Your feeling of I AM is the same as mine; there is no other. Consciousness is all One. We are all the same Being having countless separate dreams.

Enjoy the illusion of suffering and time while it lasts. It's just a fleeting moment that we created to learn and experience, and it won't last. The real magic is in our ability to make it feel so permanent. We are in fact Source Mind, deluding ourselves into believing that we are Joe Shmo so we can get out of the castle for a bit and pretend we are a commoner. Nothing could be further from the truth, and eventually all truth comes to light.

We each think of ourselves as an independent, sovereign being who stands apart from the Universe as a whole. This assumption is made from a singular point of view and does not take into account what consciousness is. The Mind can compartmentalize itself into amnesiatic self for the purpose of learning, but the truth remains: there is only one of us. The Zero-Point of all being is Oneness, and that Great Mind is the basis for all other minds. When a holographic image is broken, each chard of glass has the complete image of the original. This is us. All consciousness, the "I AM", that we are, in one and the same.

The concept of mirroring the nature of Source Mind is taught in mainstream western culture as "Created in God's Image", but this teaching falls short of telling the whole truth. You are not a distal, disconnected image of the One Mind Itself, you are it. This does not mean that you are the Big Kahuna in the flesh. That would be like putting on Grampa's shoes and walking around saying "I am Grampa!" This distinction, however, does not diminish the gravity of the realization. Your mind, your soul, is an inseparable part of the mind of that which you could call God. Your origin point is in ultimate sacredness, and to this perfect Oneness you shall return when the journey is over. In the meantime, you pretend to be you, forgetting who you really are. As Ram Das said so many times, you are God in Drag. Don't let that go to your head too much, because everybody else is too.

**The Other Side of the Coin**

The sinking feeling that we are all screwed is an idea. It is a conclusion, and like all such judgments, it is premature. The future is not here yet. It is now our time to wonder how we are going to think our way out of this perceived mess. Our solutions are still becoming clearer over time, but our current judgments are pivoting on drips of information screened through the limited ideas available at any given time. It is therefore impossible to be sure that we are all in big trouble. Whatever the truth is, it is most certainly not precisely what we have believed. So we must remain in the fluid and tenuous space of wonder.

Our basis of understanding is a snapshot in time, based on incomplete evidence. We must follow the grace of not knowing, and wonder how it's going to work out for you, and all those in your life. If you have an ounce of belief that the odds are stacked in our favor due to love's many intentions for improvement, you will soften into hopeful expectation. Knowing that love finds a way, you will look for, find and create the new version of America. This is a new version of the original dream, based on regionally focused, intelligent systems built little by little in the image of loving kindness and equal support for all. When you are on American soil, you are loved. We will live this as a people because we intend to act in compassionate support for all human beings. Let the other counties of the world once again see our beauty and ingenuity, this time with the effort of feeding, housing, and nurturing the whole human being as a matter of principle. If we keep telling everyone we are the greatest country on earth, it is time for us to act like it.

Now more divisions, no more turning a blind eye to human suffering. For this to be a reality, we must act this way ourselves, and contribute in our local communities, doing good in our immediate world. America is all about abundant American dream. While financial abundance alone once drove human behavior as the primary measurement of success, we must now wish all beings to smile and share joy, and celebrate existence. Love in its true form is unconditional and always reaching for expansion. We must step away from that which once brought us down, and apart, because it was an illusion. It wasn't real. Our dream of a kinder world is a reality within us all, and being desired, is far more likely to unfold than the undesired suffering of competition and isolation in shallow pursuits of wealth and power over other, with no regard for their wellbeing. The New Earth version of your life is concealing in your mind, and is based on a revolutionary concept of love as the basis of a just society.

Your neighborhood is your canvas. Paint your dream world based on what you know to be true about what makes humans truly and deeply happy. Make those moments happen and indulge yourself in the joy. Being afraid to be near each other is not the American Dream, and it is insane as a way of life. It drains us of our desire to exist, because is it true that we are either thriving or we are dying slowly into apathetic helpless division. Wish for all to live in bliss.

*

This new dream is a longshot, make no mistake. It is a stunt of epic proportion to trust the heart, and let love transform the world. The world portrayed in the movie "Mad Max" is always on the table for those unwilling to trust and nurture relationships. It is a possibility available through our free will to focus our way into a creation. Until it is in physical manifestation, however, it is not real. It is a fantastic creation of the mind, no more real than a Santa Suit we could put on if we choose. Thankfully, the question is never only about what is possible to visualize, it is about what is likely to occur, based on what is desired.

There are those stuck in the old ways, the warriors who want division to feast their egos on hateful content to verify their worldview of everyone being morons and criminals. This mindset, although possible, is profoundly unhelpful. It is the free of every man woman and child to think whatever they choose. We must respect the sovereignty of the human mind, and afford each to find their own way to sanity. Love is the ultimate result of sanity in its most brilliant form. Many have a very long way to go, but the truth of loves way is self-evident. In the meantime, as the grumpy ones get their act together, it is up to the rest of us to keep up our end of the bargain and remain happy anyway.

Do not feel ashamed for pursuing your bliss. Joy is profoundly unselfish because it lights up all it touches. This means that whatever programs have run in our minds to convince ourselves to complain incessantly must be examined for their validity. Given the desire for love within every mind being the perennial intention of the soul. It is our authentic, ambient vibration of our beingness. This is the feeling of the New American Way, and will become the natural state of our planet.

Each of us has a choice. We can roll and tumble and grumble, or we can let go of our angry deceit entirely, and let grace into our minds. Grace is a releasing of the grip we repeatedly find ourselves tightening, wondering if the suffering is worth it. It was pretty bad for most of us at one point, and the memory of what was is conjurable. Don't eat of that foul fruit if you want to take the leap into a better tasting life. As the trail will keep presenting thorny branches in our way, a discerning awareness traveler can find their way. Off the trail and alone has been tried and found wanting of the joy that was intended. Hand in hand, we must walk the path together, and when the beauty shows itself, we will stay from the beaten path of certainty to smell the blossoms of a new world in the making.

Alone and in fear, believing in monsters, we once clung to an unsustainable way of being. We learned that we love being around others by being isolated and we are now eager to collaborate. When we choose our focus on what can be done to expand and improve based on an open mind, we remember the True American within us. The spirit of this nation had always been based on a pioneering mindset without limitation. Those who once ridiculed will begin to support because they have run out of ideas. The old ways are inherently short of what is necessary in the fluid situation posed by modern life in this world. The fresh, brave thoughts come from the most surprising places, most often from people far younger than the leaders of the past. Our children's minds contain the blueprint of the New Earth. So far, few have listened or taken them seriously. As an aspect of humanity loves forward into an improving situation, the children's vision will lead the way.

What we used to do didn't work. The school didn't work and the lifestyle was unhealthy in almost every way. So be it. We sucked. It was a society of individuals given unloving ideas upon which we based our unloving inner reality. When we say enough is enough, we begin to allow our minds to drift into a fantasy of what a more perfect world would be like. What if kindness mattered more and money or power? What if rules that were rigid and cruel were replaced with mercy and charity, doing to others as we would do unto our loved ones? These answers are the brick and mortar of the New Earth. They exist, and they are accessible to you now for the low price of the suspension of doubt and the bravery of faith.

## The New Earth

What is meant by the "New Earth"? It is a new model of how to live, how to teach, how to distribute resources, and how to see each other, based on mutual respect and caring for all. The old model is fading away as we stop believing in it, but we must learn from our past choices as a society. The fear/greed-based culture has left too many wanting. The New Earth focuses on primary prevention, not on cleanup from a shortsighted inhumane way of living; not the glutinous manner of living that destroys our ecosystem. Those systems are falling, despite our attachments to their normalcy in our minds.

The New Earth is a life in balance. It is a society based on sustainability and the deliberate pursuit of humanitarian needs in harmony with the needs of nature. In this new social world that we are creating, it is normal to connect with natural settings, and explore the land and sea for the benefits of connection with our world. Through the inclusion of pursuits of true value, our wellbeing will soar, leading us to the next logical steps to promote more wellness in our world. Citizens of an advanced society are focused on both a inner balance and outer homeostasis, because wholistic wellness plays the long game. Beginning with the nurturing of healthy living soil and support of the many pollinators of the earth, we will help the world return to its natural, genius balance. We will now participate in the creation of healthy food, sustainable resources, and supporting our local businesses will become the natural way of living.

In addition to raising our expectations of a great life experience for as many as possible, we must also address those who have not yet learned to play well with others. The vengeance model of responding to immoral acts is going to be replaced by primary prevention model, and genuine of efforts to teach compassion for those who have drifted into an unkind mindset. Even those who break laws of country and morality are humans deserving of respectful treatment. To kill in wrathful vengeance is a never-ending cycle of insanity that teaches our children that we condone killing. The profitable prison system that was once used to discompassionately punish will be transformed into boarding schools to teach the value of love and respect for all, because compassion knows no bounds.

War is unthinkable on the New Earth, because all life is sacred. The greed, hate and fear that once fueled these conflicts will no longer be valued and accepted, replaced by ideals of a truer nature, closer to the heart. Violence is the shortsighted creation of the separated mind lost in fear and lack, and it makes no sense in a just society. Little by little, humans will choose to rescind our participation in violence, losing interest in violent entertainment, and if a few decide they need a war, nobody will show up. The weapons of greed and hate will become still and silent, because the mind of humanity has done so.

The healthcare system on the New Earth will not be driven by profit, but by results. A primary prevention model will shift the need from the old broken systems driven by greed disguised as a helping hand, and the medical community can get back to work fixing what is broken and promoting wellbeing by treating the problems at their source. We will teach about nutrition rather than medicating, and prevent long-term ailments through the promotion of a healthy, happy lifestyle. Dietary toxins will be eliminated on the New Earth, because people will matter more than productivity and profit.

The subjugation of children in the public school system designed in the 1950's will be replaced with a model that prepares people for the world as it is. We will temper of our need to evaluate and test them into compliance. The old model has placed our teachers in servitude to the pointless metrics of another time, making these bright lights dimmer in servitude to a cold, unmalleable system that does not know love. Teachers must be free to teach, and be allowed the creative exploration of a meaningful educational experience that yields balanced human beings of both virtue and wisdom. The children are the architects of the New Earth, and if the teachers and parents listen, the children's ideas will lead the way. Young humans must be nurtured in their passions, so that their natural way of being can be allowed to flow and grow. There are some things they will need to learn from us, but we have much more to learn from them. They will show us the way, when we have the courage to honor their inherent wisdom.

The goals of a humanitarian society will value the life of an individual over that of a corporation, and banks will no longer be permitted to take from the poor and give to the rich. Insufficient Funds fees, for instance, will be old lore that is shared in awe of the inhumanity of a greed based system. Taking money from someone who has none makes no sense at all if the goal is the upliftment of all. Taxation will likewise weigh more heavily on the wealthy, so that their excess can bring us all toward a moral center of all needs met. A billionaire's right to have a yacht and third home will no longer take precedence over the poor family's right to eat and have a warm home. There is plenty to go around is we stop enshrining gluttony. Filling the bellies and minds of every child on the surface of The New Earth is considered a human right.

The New Earth is a dream of a world without hate, of true equanimity, where all are free to be who they are, as they are. It is a world without judgment, where kindness naturally flows because its citizens remember the holiness of all. Those who believe in the New Earth must look for it in the places in which it is being born, and stoke the fire until all of the old is burned off, leaving nothing but the clean blue flame of the new civilization that we desire and deserve.

Doubt builds nothing, only hope can do that. Dare to believe that this is a shared dream, and in our agreement to grow in this direction as a society, it will surely become. One neighborhood at a time, one region at a time, the world is changing. It is changing because it has to, and because we want it to. The New Earth is already here in our minds, and out there in the world in drips and drabs, and occasionally, in full blown reality. Dare to hold this image in your mind, and look for it happening. Join in the motion towards, and you will be part of the becoming that some call the Ascension into the Heart.

## The Big Reset

In 2020, the world was like, OK, that happened. We broke the blooming world. The systems of business and government rattled and banged and screeched to a halt, and so did we. Years have since past, and we are all still a little shell-shocked, not knowing what is next. I now offer a perspective of an alternative interpretation to the consequences of the world spinning slowly down to die. Maybe this reset, the falling of loveless systems, will prove to be a good thing. What if the crumbling of old structures has come into our experience so we can reconceive all our systems?

Our world is long-overdue for a makeover in the image of what love wants for all of us. We have lived in a world of loveless, unkind public systems, and we didn't believe we had any choice in the matter. Therefore, we did not spend the time to envision an alternative. Our businesses were based on cold corporate scalability, and the food, schools, and the daily life of the average American was unsatisfying in almost every way. But our debtors and our fear of their power over us made us afraid. Thus, we believed we were stuck, but the chaos of change was for a purpose, unknown even to itself.

The confusion led to the now-forming reconstruction of a new model for society. Because the system is broken, we now have the window of opportunity for asserting a new societal core-priority: serving each other in a deliberate act of love, with not one human being treated as less Divine than another. The current madness is making room for love to create something brand new, a possibility of A New America. The possibility now exists for a brand new world, with a humanitarian-based society as our focus in the reforming of our governmental priorities. Unity is one for all, and all for one, mutual support, though local networks of cooperative relationships. We become good neighbors in the New Earth, in ways that are necessary, creative and kind. This is the future that ends well, the next generation of human civilization.

There is plenty of room for expansion of a humanitarian methodology loving support if we rethink the whole shebang. If we re-evaluate the value of governmental programs that protect human life, not take it, there will be plenty of purchasing power available for constructive programs to support, educate and empower each and every American. The shifting of focus from the priorities of the military industrial complex leaves ample room for new programs that serve the people. A fundimental shift is occurring in the role of government, which exists with the sole purpose of serving the wellbeing of its every citizen. By the people, for the people. The governmental structures must, therefore, serve the purpose of intelligent loving action, guided by the relevant individuals who are directly connected to the situation that desperately needs more love. This grace can be provided in more ways than thus far imagined. The helping hand must always listen to the one being helped. We must infuse grace and kindness and upliftment into all that we do together as a people, in our mutually-agreed-upon cooperative programs.

In building these new systems and programs, we will meet and share with each other our company, our connections, and our resources that flow naturally among friends. Friends are kind to each other, and Americans can be so kind and brave it boggles the mind. We carry an insightful cleverness to survive, hewn through the adventure spirit of the American Pilgrim. This spirit is within all who identify themselves as an American Citizen, it what we are. We have all huddled with our neighbors in a storm, glad for each other's company. This is the heart of what we are as a People, we take care of each other.

Let's dream a Better America into being, separately in our unique offerings of insight, connected in our purpose. We will make the world greater beginning with ourselves, acting boldly and bravely. We will also prioritize our personal needs and our individual wellbeing on all metrics, in all ways, so we can better serve the village. A starving chicken lays no eggs. The world we can create together, inspired by the will of love, is blissful wellbeing for all, as defined by the individual as the only judge of their personal experience. In our common goals, shared by many, we will create a masterful society previously conceived. We will become what our founding fathers hoped we would become: free of spirit, happy in our lives, and gracefully kind to each other.

This is the goal of America from the beginning, was to make the people even greater than before. We left old systems behind so we could build something new, a government by the people, for the people. We will continue to create new programs, together, based on what the people actually need. New-minded changes and creations will appear on a local level, built to connect human beings and bring into the world the social structures that truly help our citizens thrive. The purpose of a noble and just government is to explore what is needed and valued by the human beings who live on this land, all of them, and create what the people desire for themselves, in this time in history.

The humans who wrote our laws lived in a very different world, and some of the rules and standards were based on a reality profoundly different from the state of American right now. We must teach our children what they need to know in order to thrive in life, and cease the pointless practices of a bygone Era. The school systems of the western world have become blind to the Humanitarian needs of our most values citizens, the ones who will rule the world sooner than we realize. We must learn how to nurture creators, open-minded thinkers who are both heard and supported. They are not just our future, they are our now, our most important priority. We must rethink every assumption of the school systems, and double down on the grace and adaptability of these vital systems. We must consult them more often, because they remember what true kindness is like. The old cranky humans who have had the microphone, who seem to have lost their minds, have. They are a product of their conditioning, the result of a loveless system. It is time to stop listening to the ones who created the problems, and consult our wise children about what a better world would look like.

Washington and all our world's leaders are clearly taking their sweet time in getting their shit together, so now we have to do it ourselves. We must now work together on a local level, through our friends networks, to serve the common good. Maybe this reset is happening so we can re-conceive all our systems at the root level. There is plenty of room for expansion of a humanitarian methodology in every aspect of our society. We must infuse grace and kindness and upliftment into all that we do together in our agreed-upon societal programs. Let's dream a better America into being, with a mindset of optimism and empowerment.

Let's show the large systems how it's done by making these things happen on a local level. What does compassionate inspiration make you want to do? Do it, share it, and involve others in your creation. Then we can scale it up to the higher harmonics of global systems of aid and support to not just save lives, but enhance lives in the pursuit of holistic wellbeing. This is the New Earth that we are growing together: supportive, creative cooperation, with humans valued highly and equally, placing people before profits, with virtue as our guidance.

The mindset of the New Earth is: why not? Why not try to build new systems that are more kindly conceived? Why not dream of how life can become better because of a decision we made to try? Why not wonder how this story gets better? Why not plan based in trust that others have realized the very same things, and will surprise you in more ways than you can imagine. The New Earth is the amazing unfoldment of synchronicity because humans are learning how to tune in to our inner guidance and wisdom. Thusly, the next-level human is miracle-minded enough to be in the expectant receiving mode of synchronicities. Consequently, we will live a graceful life experience, on a higher plane of existence within the collective. A happy human is necessary for the balance, as those in suffering will need a place to dream themselves into.

The New Earth is an experience based on a mindset, made possible by an emotional experience of the indescribable connection to love's transcendent feeling. This feeling opens our personal connection to infinite wisdom. If you feel it, you are awakened in this moment. We are so glad you made it back from wherever you were that wasn't love. We've all been there, and we feel for you. It's hard on planet earth. It's heavy and dense and people keep telling you that you're late. Take off your watch and stay awhile. Take off your shoes and feel the earth beneath your feet. It is this connection that reminds you of the wisdom that flows through you in your state of connection. The New Earth is born through you in this feeling-state of connection, the vibrant creative, unified field of love. Your insights are wide and vast and powerful. In the right state of mind, anything is possible. This is where new ideas come from, from people exactly like you, in the mood of joy and wonder, dreaming of a new tomorrow.

# Part II

# Activation Thoughts

*These ideas were intended to be read more than once, perhaps aloud, for maximum effect. Withold your resistance and judgement, and just accept the sensations that these thoughts provoke, and see if you resonate with the truth that they are intended to provoke within you.*

The gravity of life's many challenges pulls hard on our souls, but with an uplifted mind, the load can be carried with grace.

*

It is natural to panic, but it is never helpful. Freaking out is just an abundance of the visualization of what might go wrong, combined with a deficiency of graceful breathing. Everybody freaks out from time to time, so don't punish yourself for being human. Just stop thrashing around in the pond of your mind and relax into silence, and let yourself begin to float back up to the surface. Inhale the possibility of improvement, beginning with the feeling of relief. This feeling is the place of constructive creation.

*

Step One: calm down.

Step Two: cheer up.

Step Three: open your mind to the best-case scenario.

Step Four: expect that.

Step Five: Live it.

89

*

The flame of insight is always eager to grow, given adequate oxygen. Breathe Big, Dream Big.

*

If you believe in an idea, it is easy to believe in yourself as you pursue it.

*

Peace begins right here; there's no place like Om.

*

We must forgive, and dare to care. We must see beyond physical distinctiveness, and love everyone as they are. We must do this because if we remain in division, in isolation and in separation, we will never know grace. Being furiously judgmental leads nowhere we want to go, because it is not a loving mindset. It is a delusion created by the ego mind to make us feel special in the illusion that others are less valuable than we are. Separation is a lie, and oneness is true.

Heal from the lie of hate, and power over and power under, of cultural norms being more important than kindness. Nothing is more important than being a loving human being to everyone, everywhere, without condition. It is a tall order, but learning how to do this is why we are here, under the false impression that only some are sacred, when in fact every one of us is a Divine Child of Source. Remember Oneness, and mutual respect is assured.

*

Speed combined with inadequate respiration results in contraction of mind that reduces the likelihood of grace and brilliance. The ability to recognize the necessity of a reduction in situational speed is the ultimate demonstration of intelligence. A smart mind notices the unpleasant feeling of being off-track, and slows down to nurture the constructive feeling of cosmic connection with Divine Intelligence, the birthright of us all.

*

Learning will continue to happen no matter what we do. It is our choice, however, whether we learn through fear or love, pleasure or pain. Listen for the soft voice of guidance, and heed the gentle warnings of when you are off-track, before they become louder and more painful. If your thoughts are bringing you down, you are off-track. If you feel eagerness and joy, love and creativity, you are clearly on track, as these kinds of thoughts are your true nature.

This is who you really are.

*

Much of the human world has become too fast and complicated to allow our wellbeing to flow. We must now reach for sanity through the slow and simple. Sit in silence, out nature, and you will know your truth. Slow down to the rhythm of the sea, get yourself together and walk in peace.

*

We can spring-board off of our repulsion, our anger and our fear, but if we are to achieve escape velocity, we must fix our eyes on the inspiring new idea that gives us hope, and stop looking back. Choose bliss, and all will unfold to your liking.

*

I am equally fascinated by the lessons that bear repeating, as well as the ones we learned from and vowed to handle very differently next time. Some teachings we look forward to forgetting, but we must remain aware of the lesson henceforth. This knowledge sets us free to create an alternative reality made possible by the crashes that we learn from and then release from our conscious thought. Forgiveness of the past, we have learned, is the key to profiting from our painful and scary lessons. Through acceptance and surrender of the old stories, we create the freedom to ascend to a higher plane of happiness.

*

Love creates the most powerful form of fearlessness the world will ever know.

*

Superficial gratification is counterfeit happiness. It feels better than despair, but not nearly as good as love. Except no substitutes.

*

Rest isn't the only way to feel better.

Veg when you need to, and then get back on your feet, and dance like no body gives a shit because they are so happy doing their own thing. That's what we get when we give ourselves to acceptance. It may not exist in all places and times, but when the music's got you, go.

Dancing is necessary for human happiness.

Move your form.

Loosen up

Let it flow in graceful motion

Love the music

And let it become part of you.

Surrender to your love of a moment, as it is.

Awaken your inner child,

and be glad for the wellbeing that flow.

Put your judgmental thoughts down for the long sleep

and dance with everybody watching,

without a care in the world.

When the time is right and the music's fine,

Set aside your resistance and

and be magnificent,

in fearless joy of being alive.

The one who danced will be uplifted.

Courage always brings forth a boost.

Turn on your lively spark, and all the Angels dance
alongside you.

Life is more fun when you try.

*

If one eats food

And needs healthy nutrition to be well,

Growing food is part of life.

Eating is not a hobby, its an occupation.

We are all farmers one way or another.

*

Eating well is the natural consequence of loving yourself.

Don't fill your body with low-end, non-O.E.M. parts. GMO is not OEM, and neither are old-school, not-nature-based chemicals of any kind. Organic food is without poison, created with love and kindness from Start to Mart. You really are what you eat.

What are the most nutritionally dense foods you can find, in season?

Dark leafy green vegetables, mineral-rich tubers, hearty beans and lots of pure water, blessed in your way. The water remembers.

Bless everything that becomes your form.

*

Forgetting is part of life

For some reason

It is easy to remember who you are when you're out in nature.

Choose to get out every day.

Put your good shoes on and get on the trail.

You know you want to.

*

Always remember that many of those of which you consider yourself appalled believes that they are a good human being.

Let compassion grow out of the grace of not knowing who anyone really is on the inside when we find ourselves becoming the blame thrower. Judgment is a double sided mirror, and it break into sharp pieces that need to be cleaned up. That is called Karma.

*

Through clarifying and sharing our creative intentions, we increase the likelihood of our dreams coming true. Some will join in your creative dream that is co-created. Not all will join in harmony, but even when others seem to be working against us, it is our own belief in the dream, and the joy we experience when we ponder it that fuels the possibility and makes it grow. If we can inspire others with our vision, we are joined in energy and the remote possibility become a likelihood. Friends make us more of who we are once we figure out who we want to be.

*

Heal yourself with grace. Move your body gently, in all directions, expanding your physical flexibility while you soften your mind into openness and peace. Yoga in all its creative forms, is how to age gracefully.

*

Each experience we have is valuable, whether it is wanted or unwanted. Like vegetables that do not make it to market, your old ideas and experiences can be recycled into the soil of your growing mind. As a gardener, we are first soil creators, then we are planters, then nurturers, and finally, we reap the harvest. There is no harvest without lively soil, enriched by the lifeforms that comprise it; in life, and in death.

Heal your soil, and watch the magic happen.

*

Fearless love in action always takes the form of grace. Love makes a most beautiful verb. The actions we feel compelled to do when we act in love are kind and caring, since we are shining the same light that Creator is shining on us.

*

Everything in the universe is temporary, which means that improvement is eventually on the way.

All is well, exactly as it is, flowing toward endless improvement. Joy always flows back in, because it is the basis of everything. Nature is joyful and abundant. It is only the human mind that can conceive of regret and shame; these concepts are not the real world.

*

Forgiveness is the sublimation of love into an environment entirely unlike itself.

*

Choose to summon the strength to endure.

*

The open mind is a holy mind. Childlike passionate curiosity is our true essence, because we are born creators. Allow your mind to wander in realms of joyful creation, because that is what we all came here to do.

*

Love sometimes results in fear, but fear cannot lead us to love. Only by finding a way to cheer up and trust that everything is going to be ok are we granted the keys to heaven.

*

Your best is getting better. Even now your dreams are coming true beneath the surface of the obvious world. The mind observes, and then the Soul asks. If it is requested with unwavering desire, in some form or another, the experience is provided.

*

The Three Questions:

1)   What is Possible?

2)   What is Probable?

3)   What is Desired?

*

The distance is closing between you and the ultimate you. All you need to do is relax into being yourself, and wait in eager hopefulness for the expanded version of you that is on the way.

*

We are better than we have ever been, and not nearly as good as we are going to be.

*

Freedom is the realization that one's mind is sovereign unto itself.

*

The softening of certainty opens the mind to more; more beneficial, mutually advantageous relationships. It is courageous trust to cooperate for mutual benefit with clear constructive intent that fixes this world. Building the systems of the New Earth will require you to invent ways to cooperate with other beings of all kinds, many quite different from you. Brave release of mistrust is required henceforth for those who wish to witness the majesty of grace.

The citizens of the New Earth will be those who believe in others.

\*

It takes a civilized human being to fix a broken world.

\*

The ones who are most in need of love are also the ones we most want to punish. Rather than continuing the cycle of justifiable cruelty, perhaps we will choose loving kindness instead. All things are either love itself, or a call to bring forth love into a situation that needs it.

\*

If someone in your field of influence is demonstrating motion that is incongruent with yours, do not allow yourself to get drawn into battle. They are just you, over there. Give your attention to both your motion and theirs. Gently, intently, move the dyadic relationship toward a beneficial demonstration of harmony of two cooperative components of a system. Briefly the two can become one in mutual honor, and thus can continue on their merry way, parting as friends of different perspectives. This is the way of grace.

*

Truth requires us to fly its flag in fearlessness, with power in our voices and love in our hearts. Some do not have ears to hear or eyes to see, and that is their sacred role in the dance. Explore what is true for you, and let others follow their own truth. With your love supporting them they are released to be as they are, and you as you are.

As genetic diversity is key to the survival of a species, as is the diversity of opinions that comprise the collective truth of humanity.

Don't judge, listen.

*

When we fall into the feeling of mundane, halfway conscious action, we become complacent. This day, every day, is brand new. This moment requires your attention. These people require your attention and your compassion. When we oversimplify the situations and people around us, we become officious and cold. We become hollow through the discompassionate enforcement of preconceived rules and expectations. In our cold enforcement, we stop acting humanly, and we lose access to grace. The feeling of being lucky, of being blessed, comes from knowing that we are walking the path of the Good Person, your way. Consequently, we let others off the cold meat-hook of our judgment. We let them be, in complete acceptance of who they wish to be.

No matter how afraid or angry we become with the world, we must not internalize it. We must now choose to turn our thoughts upward, toward gratitude of the miracles all around us. We can lift our chins up because we have felt the magnitude of suffering that comes along with poor choices and painful learning, and we see that we are no longer in that situation, and we shed that mindset. All of us have chosen fear enough to know that even when there is danger, fear is not the way. Clarity of focus on the unique situation, with belief that there is a solution, is how we find our way through the maze of life on planet Earth. Our minds are made to create solutions.

*

Love is only experienced in its fullest expression by the courageously forgiving.

*

I have many times learned who I am by walking the path of what I am not, failing to enjoy it, and then pivoting around to become congruent with the real me.

*

Self-love and self-loathing are the two lanes of the road of self-knowledge. One lane leads away from where we want to go, the other squarely toward it.

*

Fear not, the Universe wants you here. Otherwise, you would have been toast a long time ago.

*

Have the courage to exit the dimly lit cave of normalcy and bring back light to the tribe. Eventually, they will all step out into the sunshine.

*

Since we are constantly learning what we want more and less of, the improvement of the world is assured. It is awareness within contrast that clarifies our path.

*

We are all beautiful on the inside, and little by little we are allowing our insides to become outsides.

*

Life is the never-ending process of finding the sane balance between fearless freedom and neurotic paranoia. Absolute fearlessness leads to a short life on this risky plane of existence, while striving for survival above all else is a narrow, boring path that starves the soul of meaning. The middle way, once again, is wisdom.

*

What is your natural impulse when your mood is in the lighter version of you? Please elaborate.

*

Reasonable caution is an integral part of sustainable freedom, as is a touch of reckless abandon. The Source Mind with us is cheerful, creative and unpredictable. Our lively spark is a wild hair that the glum mindset will always perceive as insane.

*

In aircraft and in life, only forward motion results in lift.

*

No pilot has ever known exactly what was going to happen when they got inside their airplane. All they know is that they are going to make everything alright. Believe in the creative possibilities of your brilliant mind.

*

The faith shown by a skydiver to let go of the airplane and surrender to trust is the very same heroism that is necessary for all happiness. Allow your faith, and celebrate the moment you are experiencing as an opportunity to be the problem solver that you are. It is a blessed time, the now, and you are right smack dab in the middle of it.

*

Confidence is the child of faith and the parent of skill.

*

Those brave enough to champion the cause of loving compassion are the heroes of a time lost in shallower pursuits.

*

Fear is the only way in which slaves are held down, and therefore brave love is the means to lasting liberty.

*

All that stands in opposition to love points the way to love. It's just the other way.

*

The ability to find one dead light bulb on a Christmas tree is not as important for human happiness as the ability to replace it or ignore it. Finding fault is a distortion of our desire for safety, because perfectionism may lead to egoic gratification, but it does not lead to happiness. Rather than constantly seeking what is wrong or broken, look for the way in which you can appreciate the world as it is. Even when change is necessary, be thankful for all that resulted in the improvement.

*

Although modern life may appear to be overwhelmingly complicated, the real answer remains simple: Take care of each other, and everything will be alright.

*

The art of happiness is the ability to appreciate the positive aspects of an unchangeable situation.

*

The more we care, the greater the magnitude of negative emotion when we think in a direction counter to the values held by our higher self. The stronger the river flows, the greater the oppositional force when paddling the wrong way.

*

Relax into knowing that all is well, and on its way to better. Inner peace begins right here, right now. Breathe deep, and allow the vision of our bright future to come.

*

It appears to me now that the louder I scream "no!" at something unwanted, the more it clings to me like toilet paper on my shoe. The alternative is to give my attention to something entirely different that puts me in the better mood that leads me to the solution. Shift your vibration upwards, and the answers to the unwanted become clear, and it begins to form and drift toward us as a physical manifestation of our mind's creation. The mindset is the soil in which the plant grows. A happier mindset, therefore, will lead to more of itself.

*

When you realize that you are surrounded by negatively focused people, remember that this is an opportunity to uplift and thus be uplifted. A boat is not a boat until it is put into water.

*

Liftoff is achieved when the desire to fly is greater than the fear of crashing back to earth.

*

The only love that ever mattered is the kind without condition. We need not fear the loss of this kind of love, because it is the very basis of the human soul, and it is eternal. Nothing else is real and lasting.

*

When the human power of visualization shifts from what might go wrong to how things can go right, we will have made the paradigm shift from passenger to pilot.

*

The skydiver who is done learning is like a meteor coasting toward an inevitable impact with their unconsidered possibility.

*

Worse creates better, but better cannot be lived until the story of worse is left behind. Incessantly speaking and thinking about the undesirable past will only bring it back into the present. Learn from it, leverage it, and let it go.

*

The doorway to inner peace is never locked, but only the fearless may open it.

*

Enlightenment begins with a deep breath and a surrender to the truth of Oneness. Peel back the onion of your mind to see what is inside. Who are you, when you make the statement: "I AM."? Each of us the very same mind, standing in our unique perspective, desiring love. Oneness is truth, because despite our amnesia, we are all the same being having different experiences. We truly are One. If you feel much lighter due to this realization, you are enlightened in this moment.

*

The most insidious fear of all is the kind that results in the forfeiture of an inspired life.

*

Although we believe that the world warms our hearts, it is always we who let it in. Love is a choice. We can choose to be open and vulnerable to feel what another is feeling. We can choose to be graceful and flowing, like a tree gently swaying in the wind. Allowance is the way of grace.

*

It's not that fear is never warranted; it's just that it never solves anything.

*

Expand your lungs, expand your possibilities.

*

When fear wears out its welcome, love shows up as the only reasonable alternative.

*

The balance of power of hope and fear is tipped by shifting our focus from negative truth to positive possibilities.

*

Adventure is controlled panic interpreted as fun.

*

Forgiveness is the extrication from judgment, and thankfulness the doorway to enlightened love. This is where the Angels live, watching and hoping that we will come to where they are.

*

Although steps toward safety open the door for an easing of fear, the allowance of relief is an entirely separate event.

*

Safety in skydiving is a combination of strict adherence to consistent procedures combined with an open-minded creativity that transcends preconceived notions altogether. Rules alone are often the road to unintelligent action. Be flexible in your mind, and open to what is true in this unique moment.

*

Freedom is not free, but the cost need not be war. The real cost is the perilous release of fear to allow one to occupy liberty in all its wondrous forms. Freedom without courage is short lived.

*

Rise upward above the battleground of the ego, and put it all to rest. Struggling and fighting as a way of being creates too much collateral damage in our hearts. The battle always costs us the truthful perspective of Oneness. When we believe in good and evil, right and wrong, good guys and bad guys, we split the world in two, and thus enter into the illusion of separation. There is only the desired world, and the world that made us desire it, one process that reveals the truth of who we want to be.

*

Every time a person or a society strives to simplify the brilliant rainbow of human experience, they find themselves in the darkness. Freedom is fearless acceptance of all that humanity is, was, and will be. Let go of judgment and accept. They are you, in that lane, doing what makes sense to them.

*

Joyful appreciation is not just the result of things going well, it is also the reason for things going well. Vibe Matters.

*

Danger creates both fear and wisdom, and if you wear it well, happiness.

*

It is the treating of others as objects that results in the marginalization of love in a world in dire need of it. Even if you don't understand another person's ways, they are real people with a perspective that is valid for them. Honor their journey, wish them well, and stay in your lane. You have a job to do, as do they. Let the wheels turn on their own, because you don't know what role they are playing in the evolution of human consciousness.

*

The fact that there is sound reason to panic is not an excuse to do so. The mind thinks its way into fear, and grace guides us out of it.

*

The state of grace begins with a feeling of appreciation for the present moment just as it is.

*

Although improvement is always on the way, we must first appreciate the value of our here and now if we are to graduate to there and then.

*

Profundity is born from a focus on the amazing, the painful, and the mundane. Compost your life, every bit.

*

Love is the greatest gift of all for our learning, because it brings us face to face with the very source of fear, a separation from love. Delightfully, love itself is the answer to the fear that it produces.

*

Just as every high voltage line needs to be grounded, the higher the level of danger, the greater the need for release and inner peace. All rituals that bring us to silent peace are a step in the right direction, as long as the intention is clear to let go of what was, and be with that is. Settle down, breathe and accept, then stand tall in your actions taken with a calm core within your mind.

*

The fear of greatness makes us meek, and the fear of meekness makes us great.

*

The fear of appropriate aggression can render the loving impotent. Skillful anger is the harbinger of change that will reshape our world into a larger receptacle of love. Kindness comes in many forms, and sometimes love is a blazing fire that burns away that which is not loving. To be truly powerful, we must embrace all that we are, including our anger.

*

There is a difference between anger and hatred. We are all in the process of learning the balance between destructive anger and productive anger. There is a time to get pissed off, and it is the harnessing of this power that is at the heart of becoming a complete human being. Even when your eyes become red, your breath can control the burn so that your heart can guide your head.

*

A snake was told by the Buddha, "Do not harm anyone." A group of boys found the snake sunning himself on a rock, and in their fear, beat him within an inch of his life. He slithered back to the Buddha to show him what had happened. Looking lovingly upon the injured snake, he said: "I didn't tell you not to hiss!"

*

There is a difference between fear and caution. Caution takes well thought-out steps that increase the actual level of safety, whereas fear results in unintelligent knee-jerk reactions that make us feel worse because they lead away from both safety and freedom.

*

The willingness to tolerate the uncomfortable sensation of fear is a prerequisite for all greatness.

*

Enlightenment cannot be forced. We need to be in the vicinity of an insight to get wind of it. If you are primed for an "Aha!", and you place yourself in extraordinary circumstances, you are more likely to have an extraordinary experience.

*

The ability to reach for joy amidst terror is the very heart of adventure. The inability to shake the fear, on the other hand, is the source of misadventure.

*

When logic is unable to peel back the icy grip of fear, humor is always available to do the impossible. In the immortal words of Wavy Gravy: "If you don't have a sense of humor, it just isn't funny."

*

When the speed and complexity blows your hair back in abject terror, WOOHOO seems to be the magic word.

*

We all have faith. It's just that many people put more faith in illness than in wellness, more belief in poverty than in the hope of abundance, and more confidence in hate than in love. As with all things, we tend to get what we believe.

*

Many blame the media for chewing the cud of the horrible, and thus promoting a feeling of fear in our society. Although this may be true, it will always be our choice what we give our attention to, and thus how we feel is still up to us.

Make no mistake, I am not suggesting that we need to live with our heads in the sand in order to be happy. The fear-provoking information about the world is how we draw forth the ways to make things better. We cannot, however, do this from a feeling of overwhelment. When your observation of the disproportionate media is throwing you out of your optimistic place of power, remember that selective focus is your birthright. We are all free to change the channel or turn it off in order to get back into the mindset that allows us to observe things that need improving and remain in a place of powerful creativity to launch the new ideas of a better world. Remain steadfast in your power by walking away from that which mutes your light. The peaceful warrior alternates between service to the Light and sitting in silent repose in nature, being one with everything. Remembering what we are fighting for is what gives us the strength to continue onward.

*

It is possible that there are people who would prefer you to be afraid because it gives them more power. It is also true that we are becoming too smart for that, and our intelligent compassion will shine through anyway. If nobody buys what they are selling, they will go out of business.

*

The universe is incredibly creative in the kinds of challenges it hands us for our soul's evolution. We must be smart in the way we respond. Remember that fear causes hypoxia, and so breathing equals brains.

<u>Slow is Beautiful</u>

Silence is the heart of music.

Stillness, the origin of grace.

When we stop and be quiet,

the beauty shines through.

Fear comes from an unsettled mind,

orbiting around the unwanted.

The silent mind cannot fear,

because it orbits around nothing.

Now take a deep breath, smile, and become Grace.

\*

The reset button is always there to return us to a feeling of relief and openness to better possibilities. All we need to do is borrow a big breath of sky into our lungs, and slowly, ever so slowly, set it free.

\*

Much of the world's crankiness and aggression could be alleviated by friends reminding friends to breathe bigger and slower. Give your friends and loved one's permission to remind you to become yourself again. As taught in <u>A Course in Miracles</u>, my safety lies in my defenselessness.

\*

Since worse always causes the summoning of better, there is no reason to fear that the present conditions will remain forever. It always changes, and it improves specifically because of what has been before. The shadows are where the light wants to shine.

\*

In life, either you are a directed specific or a wandering generality. Purpose is Power: Intend.

*

Diagnosing the problem is always step one in reaching for improvement, but all too often we get stuck in this phase rather than moving ahead into the answer we have realized. Finding fault is not the same as creating and becoming solutions. Lining up with success always feels better than finding more reasons why we cannot succeed.

*

When we are not having fun, slowing down and clearing our heads is an important part of the cheering up process. We must make room for better by increasing the space between our ears.

*

Fear is far too dangerous an emotion to spend more than a few seconds pondering, but without glimpses of the undesirable, we cannot avoid it and reach for its glorious opposites.

*

The answer to fear is often as simple as allowing our laughter. Lighten the weight of your mind by turning the solid into humor.

*

Skydivers survive because we take care of ourselves, and each other. Safety is the natural consequence of love.

*

Fear is not the source of danger, but excessive attention to negative imagery magnifies the negative possibilities. Fear is what makes danger dangerous.

*

Envisioning safety is always the first step toward survival. Visualization is not just an inconsequential dream of possibilities, it is the pre-unfolding of reality, and is every bit as real as the physical manifestation that follows. The body cannot go where the mind has not gone first.

*

Adventure is not an activity but a state of mind that reaches for greater joy at the risk of greater pain.

*

The goal of the optimistic mind is the best-case scenario rather than just following through with our first thought. Unexamined limitations are the product of a mind imprisoned in fear.

*

The economic shift is not about moving from recession back to abundance, although that will be one of the benefits. The new paradigm is about pursuing life avenues that feel better, and allowing happiness lead us to abundance of a deeper nature. The New Earth is based on authenticity of purpose, because passion is the abundance that we desire above all else.

*

Nature favors those driven by what is right, rather than by what feels safest. Wisdom plus bravery equals fitness.

*

Regret is the way in which we avoid profiting from failure. Everything has a positive aspect that leads to improvement in the future.

*

We are creators, but we often squander this power by dwelling on what is. This is the systemic disease called "what-is-itis", and it can only be cured by bravely focusing on the image of better that we do not yet see with our eyes. To dream of more than what is before us and fearlessly reach for it, this is the true nature of humanity's spirit, and the source of our authentic happiness.

*

Most people do safe things dangerously to get a rush.

Adventurers prefer to do dangerous things safely.

Its not about the adrenaline, its about the happiness.

*

The stock market is merely a reflection of the emotion of the times. All emotions can be improved upon, as how we feel is a choice about what we give our attention to. "What is" does not have to be the only focus of attention. What can be is a much more interesting conversation.

*

When we transform our fears into our concerns, we flow in a river of solutions.

*

Happiness will always be the best defense against danger.

*

The pursuit of mastery within the realm of risk is where we stoke the fire of the human spirit.

*

A life with too much risk is often too short, but a life without risk is no life at all.

Life is fear versus trust. Fear brings us less of what we hate and none of what we love. Trust brings us some of what we hate and everything that we love.

*

One cannot simultaneously prepare for the worst-case scenario and the best-case scenario, each prevents the other.

*

Abbreviated Owner's Manual for the mind: If you are not enjoying the thoughts that are in your head, change them, before they change you. We become what you think.

*

If it doesn't feel good, you aren't doing it right.

*

Fearless conviction to a good idea is the way of genius.

*

Invest in passion. It pays bigger returns than fear.

*

Do not be afraid of success if you want to experience it.

*

Fear is like a good friend who chooses a path that you would not choose to walk. You do not judge them. You do not join them. You just love them and go your own way.

*

Whatever life hands you, there is a better way to see it than the way you see things when you first look. Your fear has shown up because you are thinking about the negative possibilities that you saw in your first glance at the situation. When you are on the lookout for how things can go better, you are more likely to find success.

*

The process of transcending fear is the business of happiness itself.

*

I love humans, even when we are scared and selfish, we are able to shake it off and do the right thing. Unarguably, we are far easier to appreciate when we are aren't being shmucks to each other, but the amount of love that we radiate into the universe is greater than the amount of fear. The best part is, the love-level is still climbing.

*

Fear limits the expansion of the human heart, and the degree to which its intentions are carried out. A fearful mindset is thusly selfish, uncreative and narrow-minded. I am therefore against it as a way of being. Love connects us to each other and to the compassionate view of ourselves that nurtures our inner being. I am therefore in support of all things loving, because love supports the interconnection of the world and all the beings that live here.

*

What if everything was going to be ok? What would that look like? Are you brave enough to think in that direction until it is reality?

*

Until you have the courage to let yourself surrender to the brave task of envisioning the story of things going well, you are destined to walk another path. The world is born in the mind.

*

When you remember how lovable the human species can be, you will stop fearing them and start believing in them.

*

You can let go of the fear that you are the only one who freaks out from time to time. Separation and isolation are a lie, and illusion created by the ego to justify its apparent existence. What makes us real is connection, not separation.

*

Courageously thinking something other than the valid reasons to worry, this is the art of being happy. If it is not in your direct experience, it is not yours to attend to. Stay in your lane, and do your job of radiating joy to the world.

*

The process of relaxing is the process of rejoining with the best version of you, and all the good that it entails. Every deep breath is sacred. Every grin is a star being born. That sparkle in your eye is your true essence. Love powerfully against the dying of the light.

*

Love always eventually triumphs over fear, although sometimes you have to be a little patient. The worse anything gets, the greater the pull in the other direction. This is the physics of the universe. Things eventually get better, because the intelligent design of the Universe is YOU.

*

If you consider what modern quantum physics is saying about the nature of matter itself, you will inevitably draw the conclusion that you are more in control over your life than you ever thought possible, in more ways than you previously believed. Once you accept this, all you need to do is shed your resistance, and any experience is within your reach.

It is all energy.

*

If you can't see how ridiculous you look when you are afraid, you cannot step out of the experience. If, however, you realize that you were just thinking in the wrong direction, you will just laugh and look the other way.

*

All you need to do in order to shed your fear is start looking for the way, and stop looking back. Flip your fear upside down, laugh at it, love it to death, and do what the specific distaste suggests in terms of action for improvement. If there is nothing you can do to change what is, your job is forgiveness and acceptance. Truth often sounds way too simple, but it is what it is.

*

Life, much like flight, is the ongoing experience of breathing our way out of frozen terror to enable our flowing awareness in a sovereign act of creation. When a change of paradigm occurs, a human being will naturally respond first with paralysis in fear, then softening through the Zen mindset of peace, we naturally expand into playful, creative brilliance. Humanity's most joyous potential exists within the possibility of each individual realizing that they want to create experiences which are congruent with who they really are. This is what makes one a realized being. Each has their own version of the ascending stairway to the heaven of a happy mind.

*

Although we have learned how to be nice through some painful lessons, the good deeds of the human species far outweigh the messes we have made. We are merely children learning about love.

*

Fear is just a poke that points you in the direction you want to go. It is only when we poke back that things get ugly.

*

If our goal is to be happy, then fear is clearly counter to that goal, because it makes us feel lousy. Fear is the exact opposite of happiness, but it shows us the danger that would make us even more unhappy. Take the information and put it to good use. Keep in mind that the memos we receive about danger are written on flammable paper. Don't use the intel to light your inner world on fire. Just take the wisdom and run.

*

I love witnessing people acting heroically. They see the big picture, act with their hearts, and ignore their previous programming. This is called doing the right thing. It is when humanity shows its true nature.

*

Getting your panties in a bunch is not the way to get you where you want to go. That comes from fixing what needs fixing and having a good time along the way.

*

If we choose to focus on all the good things that humanity has achieved throughout our journey on this earth, we will not fear for our future.

*

We are the most insightful species on this planet. We are the ones who will fix everything, little by little, and continue on the infinite path toward better. It's what we do. Our capacity for abstract thought makes us the stewards of the Earth, and the creators of the future. All the other species are relying on us to get our act together. When we are stricken with fear about the seemingly monumental task of maintaining the homeostasis of an entire world, all we need do is remember how good things actually are flowing all on their own, and focus our energy on being thankful. That is how we connect with the many solutions facing our planet. When we look for the balance, the flow, and the wellbeing, we know how to facilitate these processes, and how to get out of the way.

*

When we are alone, we are filled with fear of commitment.
When we are in love, we fear the loss of what we have.
When we are poor, we fear success.
When we are wealthy, we fear becoming impoverished.

When we enjoy being alone, we don't worry about commitment.
When we enjoy being in love, we have no time to think about the relationship ending.
When we stop making our lack of money a reason to be unhappy,
we celebrate simplicity,
When we are thankful for our abundance, our inner feeling

of worthiness allows it to continue.

\*

Fear is the very bottom of the emotional scale. It is the sub-basement of the soul. Fortunately, Love is an elevator that goes all the way to the top floor.

\*

Money is just another reflection of the universal oscillation, the ebb and flow between love and fear. It is the choice of the storyteller to either weave a tale about how well things are going versus the story about how we are going broke.

Poverty is a state of mind, as is abundance.

\*

If you are afraid to be yourself, you can't sell anybody anything, because you are nobody.

\*

A sigh of relief is the sound of things getting better.

\*

If you are less afraid of running out of money than you are excited about being successful, you are on your way.

\*

When your resistance to love is set aside, you are your true self. Why resist what you have wanted all along?

Be tender.

Be kind and gentle and giving.

Forgive and ask for forgiveness when you have acted without love.

Intend love, think loving thoughts, speak love, and act out love's will. What does love think of this, of her, of him, of them?

This mindset is the One Mind that connects us all.

*

All over the world, ordinary people are choosing fearless freedom over restriction. It is the quickening of humanities' journey from doing what we are told is right, to feeling what is right and acting upon that. It is the leaving behind of things we don't actually believe in favor of things that we know to be true in our hearts. This is the dawning of the Age of Heroism, the Time of Inner Freedom. Celebrate!

*

The process of working with your fear is the most important work you are doing on this planet. It is how you peel back the layers of culture and false beliefs about yourself, and allow your inner groovy to spill forth.

*

Hate is just another aversion that is easily dissolved in a moment of compassion. Humanity is capable of awakening love in a single instant, because the desire to do good was there along, waiting for an opportunity to come out. We are all heroes waiting for our moment in the sun, and nothing shines brighter than love.

The problem that keeps coming up is the fact that we are often too cranky to seize the moment when it comes. When we waste our time complaining, we get in our own way of being as amazing as we intended to be. Your dominant areas of focus are your signal to the Universe that you wish to create more of this. Complaining is just another way to demonstrate our power to create the content of our minds.

*

On Suffering:

The worse it gets, the better it will feel when it stops sucking.

*

You cannot let your reasons for being freaked out freak you out.

*

It is in the moments when we are lost in negative experience that we require the memory of what it is like to be happier than this.
Once you accept that,
things are inevitably going to get better.

Remember and rekindle your Original Happiness.
*

Daring to feel compassion and help others is a sure sign of fearlessness. It takes a massive set of gonads to care, and apathy is the worst kind of cowardice. Love requires us to grow a pair.
*

You must find your own way back to happiness, since it is always you who sent you away in the first place. When you decide to let go of your fear of what everybody else will think if you are happier than they are, you will tap into the never-ending source of life energy called fearless joy. When you shine that light on another, you earn your keep in this world.

*

Notice how beautiful our species can be when we are not driven by fear. Notice the generosity of spirit of a child, and you will remember who you are. We are just children, later.

*

When we think with our hearts, we are fearless in a way that goes beyond the physical bravery of a mountain climber, pilot or soldier. When we do what is right, despite our knowledge of the dangers, we are being who we were meant to be.

*

You know you can be more than this. You have seen your true colors. All you need to do is look away from your fear, and let your freak flag fly.

For instance: If you know that you want a garden, and your homeowner's association tells you that you are not allowed to have one, you have two choices. You can lie down and let things be as they are, and in avoiding confrontation, you sacrifice your freedom and wellbeing. That is what many people will do. This is the way of fear. The more powerful choice is to ignore what other people will do, and plant your seeds anyway. Perhaps you will knock on doors and spread the word of a necessary change to the rules. Perhaps you will make a difference in your present community, or perhaps you will move to the countryside and build a massive organic garden. Perhaps you will help create a community garden for all those who do not have the land to sow their seeds. One thing is for certain, if you do nothing, nothing changes. The powerful are compelled to take right action despite the fear of ridicule and shame and resentment of those who do not understand. The way of fearlessness is the way of true freedom.

*

Does anything feel better than reexamining your aversions and finding gems within them? Do you have embedded beliefs that your aversion has caused? Are you realizing that these beliefs are untrue? Are you making a choice to let go of the lies in your mind that keep you small and in fear? A repulsion is merely information that clarifies who you are and what you believe. Notice and examine the unconscious processes of your mind, and explore a more loving way to think, feel and be.

*

You are brilliant, creative, and your true mind is based in absolute freedom. It is time to rise up and be the full self that your old self could not hold within it. It was just too

136

small a container. Your true nature is expanding all the time, and at some point you have to go with freedom. When you realize who you really are, the freedom of expansion is the only reasonable choice.

*

Humanity is faced with a choice. On one hand we have fear, and on the other we have love. Which one you choose in each moment determines who you are becoming. Each act is another opportunity to show who you wish to be. I beg you, choose love.

*

There are a great many reasons to feel fear, and many of them are valid. The belief in the beneficiality of the thoughts that fear leads us to is the real fallacy.

*

The Inner You is not in question. It never was. You are perfect just as you are. The problem comes when you conform through fear, and act in a manner contrary to who you really are and what you truly believe in. This is the root of all illness and suffering in the world. When you let yourself flow with the nature of your true self, all is absolutely well.

*

When faced with a big decision, fear will always present an option that feels safer, but leads you away from the right path. Even when a course correction is necessary, it is not your fear that guides you, it is your wisdom to know the way.

*

Inner peace does not come from external circumstances, but in a choice to allow the feeling of relief, regardless of the circumstances. Even more accurately, peace comes from the remembrance that you are peace, and you always were.

*

A society's relationship to fear and risk is what determines its overall success. A brave culture that strives for all that is right will not dwell on the possible consequences to failure, but will instead focus its attention on the sole prospect of reaching for something better.

*

We are brave. It is who we are. To act differently would be contrary to our true nature. When we act meekly, the source of our pain is the comparison between who we really are and who we are being. Nothing causes more suffering and depression than knowing that you can be larger than you are being.

*

You do not need to reach for what you believe in, it is your freedom as a sentient being to choose something else. You are so free that you can choose bondage to misery. But when you have had enough of the inner turmoil that comes along with taking the cowardly path, you will realize that the brave way is the only you.

*

The longer you live outside of your ideals, the more you are able to love life when you surrender to being who you really are. Appreciation comes from contrast. The backdrop of distaste is the only way in which we learn the truth. Repulsion always bears the gift of clarity. Either it is the foreground or the background, but it is all part of the picture.

*

Even in the hardest times, it is our fear that keeps us from coming together and doing what most needs to be done: Pot-luck suppers and singing songs in the darkness. When you fearlessly open yourself to your subsistence community, you find everything you need. Stone soup, baby.

*

Are the opinions of others more important than allowing you to be you? Although most of us do not believe that we are driven by our fear of what others think, the vast majority are in strict conformance with the norm. Someone is lying to themselves, and it's not the weirdoes.

*

Even one who has been driven by fear their entire lives can make a choice to turn the corner and shake off the old ways of worry. It is just a shift in thought. We are always free to do whatever makes the most sense, and fear is senseless.

It is not the altitude that gets a skydiver to that feeling of bliss, it is their fearless attitude of joyful celebration.

*

Happiness is the solution to fear. When we allow joy, the answers that create safety appear in our minds, because we become congruent with the solution.

*

The feeling of relief is always the first step away from negative emotion and toward bliss. If you have been driving your car in reverse, you must first stop in neutral before moving forward. For many of us, the "N" on the dashboard is not neutral, it is Nature. Go to the forest and find your sustainable pace. Connect with grace. Breathe with the trees, and listen to the ways of the real world. The forest is not experiencing stress, and it does not worry. It simply is, and in its simple acceptance of itself, happiness abounds.

*

Surrendering to the process of getting happier is always a heroic act, especially when you are surrounded by people who are not currently happy. Daring to be happy enough to annoy the miserable folks is one of the healthiest goals in life. It is not to do them harm, but to stand as a brave example of joy.

*

If you are driven by fear, you can only discover and create more things that make you afraid. Like attracts Like.

*

The courage we muster in times of physical danger are preparation for the courage required when we know in our gut that a change to the world is required for love to be served.

*

He who fears nothing, loves nothing. Even the enlightened mind will fear the loss of what is loved, because being in human form requires components of the egoic consciousness to stay alive. You are both Spirit and Form, and you would be insane to expect all attachment to just dissolve just because you know that you are one with everything. Feel no shame in your fear, it is part of you. Love the whole mind, the expansive and the contracted, because it is all you. That said, you don't need to give the microphone to the most panicked part of your mind.

*

I believe that evolution once favored the brave for their strength and their willingness to fight for survival. Those days, in a literal sense, are mostly in the past. Now the game has shifted to a different kind of bravery, what might be called Heroism of the Heart. Connecting and cooperating with other people, and daring to share how we really feel, these are the things that will show up most in humanity's future as "Beneficial Adaptations". In this next phase of human evolution, imaginative loving compassion will be selected as the most desirable of traits.

*

Love is the most heroic pursuit that we will ever undertake.

*

People need to stop being afraid of each other. Trust is a leap of faith, and leap we must if we are to be anything but alone.

*

Daring to thrive in the context of others suffering, this is bravery. Shed the guilt and shame for being a survivor. Someone's got to do it. You can't hold your breath to give someone else more air.

*

Your past is unchangeable, and from a certain perspective, so is your present, as the now is constructed in the past. It is only your future that is within your control. Dream it bravely.

*

If you aren't afraid from time to time, you aren't expanding.

*

Who are you when you forget your fear?

*

Doing something dangerous that does not scare you is not true bravery. It is when we forge ahead despite our personal panic alarms that makes us heroes.

*

Real love is the unconditional experience of limitless compassion that comes as a result of focusing on the most positive aspects of another person. As we give our undivided attention to their beauty and brilliance, we magnify it, and they shine even brighter. This is how fearless love creates the evolution of the soul: Friendship.

*

Love, wherever it goes, leads us in the direction of more of itself.

*

It may be so that there is much to fear, but if we fearlessly band together and help each other out, there is no need to be afraid.

*

A deep slow breath followed by a relief-filled smile seems to be the solution to most of life's obstructions. A new perspective from a higher altitude yields a plethora of new possibilities. Rise up above the battleground.

*

Love is the cause of both fear and heroism. These seeming polarities are opposite ends of the same stick. There are no opponent forces, only cooperative systems of balancing forces. It is heroic to see the wholistic oneness in everything.

*

In the process of visualizing the specifics of things going as well as possible for ourselves and for the ones we love, we find ourselves thinking brave, constructive thoughts. This is the magical creativity that love causes, with its uncompromising drive toward what is best. Love causes human bravery with a creative twist.

\*

All the world's suffering and confusion could easily be abated if each one of us would take five minutes a day to go sit on a rock and smile. Me time serves all of us.

\*

Fear is simply gazing in a direction you didn't want to go anyway.

\*

Isn't it funny that we find it harder to share our joy than it is to complain about things that aren't working? The dominant conversation might be bitching, but what creates more joy is the celebration of the positive aspects of our reality. Let them whine, and go be the celebrator you were meant to be.

\*

Loving life requires us to push into the realms that provoke our fear, and when we focus on the joy of the process, the lemon is always worth the squeeze. Danger is forced awakening.

\*

When you remember that everything is on its way to better, you will take a deep breath, let go of your struggle and allow your outer smile to light the way to your inner truth.

*

Waiting to feel relief for when better circumstances arrive is formula for prolonged crankiness. Feel bliss now, and the world will wrap around the sensation to create a corresponding reality.

*

Relief can flow in whenever we allow it. Once we do, our resistance subsides and the improved conditions that we desire show up much faster. It is not surprising that we get cranky when we focus on the aspects of our lives that are not to our liking. That is our emotional guidance system doing its job, telling us that we are off track. However, all of our power to create improvement stems from our alignment with our higher selves. Although our response to the idea of cheering up in the middle of the crisis is most often: "I don't have time to cheer up!", in truth, we don't have time NOT to cheer up. We create what we are.

*

Milk it when you are in the zone, and let go and focus in a more general way when you are not feeling the love. When we are bumming out about something, getting more specific only magnifies the negative emotion because we are focusing in a way that our higher selves would not. Let go, and allow your cork to float again. Well-being is the natural state of consciousness. It always returns if we stop justifying our misery.

*

True courage can only be attained by those who are first held back by fear, and then decide that freedom is more important than safety. Moving up the emotional gradient always feels good, especially when were briefly thought we were screwed.

*

The past is not who you are, it is just what you did. You are better than you have evidence to support. The data is just what happened, while intention is who you really are.

*

If you can find a way to love it, you will no longer fear it.

*

Profiting from experience requires a lightness of heart when reviewing our failures. If you cannot laugh, you cannot learn.

*

It is not our limitations that define us, but our constant expansion toward who we are when we express our true beauty.

*

There is plenty of evidence in both directions, so we might as well make our case that everything is going to work out fine. What we expect is what we get.

*

The beauty of humanity is not our perfection but our imperfection. We are on a never-ending journey toward better, clarified by worse. There is no perfect, only inspired expansion on the way to perfection.

*

Although humanity has been trying to complain its way into improvement for some time now, evidence suggests that this does not work. The squeaky wheel only attracts more to squeak about.

*

No matter how bleak things may look, there is always a thought that turns the corner for you. The long list of things that you love are your best defense against that which brings you down. Look where you want to go.

*

The only thing that can consistently lift us above our fear is our trust in the universal forces of well-being that flow to us in every moment. When we allow our worthiness, we allow our true heroic nature because we become congruent with the beneficial flow that is life. The Universe wants you to thrive.

*

If you can't land your parachute exactly where you want to, eventually you will land someplace you really don't want to. Skill is safety, and knowledge is lift.

*

Life is the inspiring comparison between what we prefer and its many opposites.

*

The wider the birth we take around danger, the less we learn in life. As we get closer to the danger, however, the lessons become less and less the kind we want to repeat. Our emotional guidance system shows us the way.

*

There is nothing worth sacrificing your good mood, because all of your power and wisdom to improve your current situation is born within your positive emotion. Don't trade your authentic smile for anything.

*

Those who count their blessings, find their blessings.

*

Children are born hopeful, playful and brilliant because that is who we really are. Negativity and limitation are just the effects of valuing the opinions of others over our own inner wisdom and natural well-being. Remember who you are.

*

Positive emotion is the yes within us that turns hope into luck.

*

The beauty and value of this very moment is the doorway to your enlightenment. Appreciation is the key to grace. Thank you, thank you, thank you...

*

When happiness becomes disengaged from conditions, our lightness of spirit always transforms our circumstances.

*

The manifested reality around you is merely a symptom of your past patterns of emotional fixation and beliefs. If you choose to conjure the feeling of how you want the future to be, you are always destined to live in happiness, because it all begins right here, right now. Visualization is creation.

*

Who is the happiest version of you? What words would you use to describe the real you, when you are unlimited by fear?

*

All negative emotion has the potential to inspire improvement, although most often it is mind-looped and consequently results in more experiences that lead back to itself. Notice it, learn from it, and return to your original, innate happiness.

*

Prolonged fear is inversely proportional to intelligence, compassion and wisdom.

*

The opposite of fear is freedom to be the real you.

*

It is never too late to be the optimistic one. Pivot, and wonder how things can go well. Like really, really well.

*

Having an unhappy moment is always a consequence of thinking a thought that the real you would never think. We can always look upon our circumstances in a new way.

*

When we fear for the ones we love, we stop radiating the feeling of love. Only love sends love.

*

It is the emphasis on the distinction between seeing with our eyes and seeing with our minds that weakens our power to create beyond the given world. Remember how to use your imagination.

*

The best version of you is yet to come, and when you feel great, you have your confirmation that you are heading in that direction.

*

The emotional guidance wisdom fuels us with positive emotion when we are on track, and fills us with negative emotion when we are framing our reality in a way that our higher selves would never do.

*

Half-truths are the most enticing wrong paths. They draw us in and then they make us feel bad. They lead us astray, to an untrue perspective that brings down the vibrational emanation, and thus our pattern of attraction. Reach for the purest truths that you can access. Reach with your whole mind and body as your means of discernment, and hold above all a query into the validity and connectivity that this idea serves.

When an idea is one of judgment and separation, lack and disdainful disgust, immediately ask yourself the following:

Is it true?

Is there a perspective in which this is not true, that is more loving?

If so, abandon the concept as not of your own mind, but of the socially programmed stereotypical thought patterns of the trained mind. If many others would respond in the same way, with the same distain, you are playing out a program. All that is not love is not you. Study your mind with gentle grace, notice it and hold all thoughts lightly in the palm of your hand. Only own that which you are.

You are the joy, the grace, and the knowing that love is the way.

*

When the emphasis is on enjoying the process of your expansion, all of the journey is the summit.

*

Progress is not facilitated by taking score of the past or present, but in the up-slope drift of emotions toward our primary objective, happiness. Wherever you are, wherever you are going, finding a way to be happy right now is the only path goes where you want to go. It may require awakening to beliefs that were making you miserable for a long time, and that process is the best kind of work. It unloads your burdens of the untruth in your mind, allowing your true perspective to shine the way to bliss.

*

Make your own vibe. When you choose your emotions, you choose your life.

*

The mindset that finds fault is rarely the mindset that creates improvement. Complaining are not fixing, and fixers rarely complain.

*

Life balance is about percentages. If you spend 90 percent of your time isolating problems and justifying why things can't change, you are a complainer. If you spend 90 percent of your time talking and thinking about the new and improved version of the world, you are a visionary creator. Fortunately, we can always recognize when we are being a complainer and switch gears whenever we want to by changing our focus of thought and conversation.

*

Bravery and love are the doorway to all lasting freedom.

*

Through our appreciation of the miraculous nature of the mundane, we spin the wheel of amazement to further inspire ourselves with the desire for more. This is a magical world for the miracle-minded.

*

The positive future is created by the negative past. Conscious processing is a compost that turns yuck into yum.

*

There is no point so important that we need to leave love out of the conversation.

*

When the fear of the judgment of others is superseded by the joy of being alive, we flow downstream with the current of our beautiful true nature. Only the glad truly live.

155

*

Why waste energy complaining about the unchangeable when you can benefit from celebrating the upside of your time and place?

*

Happy people are always easier to love because they are in connection with the ways in which they are lovable.

*

Friendships are the most important aspect of life. Nothing helps us to find ourselves quite like the perspective of those who love us. They see you, and they still love you. That says something. Can you see what they see?

*

If you can find a way to find delight in your very own shoes right where you are, you have won. The kingdom of heaven is always right here, right now.

*

Addiction is the belief that you need something outside yourself to be happy. Transform your perception of your addictions into preferences that you can either engage in, or not. The locus of control, the beingness of joy, is within you, not out there.

*

Holistic wellbeing begins and ends with a choice to enjoy your life to the fullest. The feeling of joy leads to everything you need, because the mindset of happiness is fundamentally productive.

*

Inspiration is a natural consequence of living. We walk our paths, and the contrast between our experience and our preferences leads us to powerful desires. It is the willingness to tenaciously look beyond the current state of affairs and toward our dreams makes us visionaries. Inspire yourself through the journey of your experience, and be proud of who you are.

*

The difference between simply being alive and a life worth living is fearless dedication to purpose. Only you know what your purpose is, and only you are able to judge whether or not you are cowering away from your path. Fortunately, it is never too late to return to a life with meaning. Look for the sparkle of joy, and follow the light to your way of joy.

*

Have a light heart as you ease off of the feeling of negativity that was caused by focusing only on the downside of this situation, and let the feeling of relief in. Like a wheel beginning to slow to a stop and then spin the other way, you are re-entering the realm of constructive appreciation. You have returned home.

*

Where fear and euphoria overlap is the place called happiness. Enjoy your fear, and it will not control you.

*

Expansion is always a little uncomfortable, but it is always worth the stretch.

*

Keeping it together when the poop hits the prop is partly about focus, partly about breathing, and partly about finding a way to enjoy the ride. Lean in.

*

We are not here to just take up space, or to live as long as possible. We are here to expand that which has been before, and reach out for our dreams in childlike expectation of their creation. We cannot let fear stop us from being the powerful creators we were born to be.

*

There is no bravery without fear, but when the desire is strong, the fear becomes weak. Inspiration is the source of all heroism.

*

Having the guts to tell your friends how much you appreciate them is how good friends become great friends. Bravery begins with metaphorical challenges of a physical nature, but we are just training ourselves for the risks that matter most. Love is heroic.

*

Without dreams, we are just shells, containers without purpose. We were born to dream, and then live those dreams. The arrival is gratifying, but the journey there can be just as blissful to the enlightened dreamer. Savor your vision, even before it comes into form. Being non-physical does not make it any less real.

*

Shedding the fear of our differences is what opens the door for all the best that life has to offer. Celebrate the diversity of the human experience. Every journey has its value to a Universe discovering itself through you.

*

I love skydivers. While most people are crazy pretending to be sane, skydivers are most often the sanest people I have met. Crazy...

*

Gravity sports are a truly beautiful creation. We are forced by danger to focus completely on the present moment. Thus, we re-emerge into a feeling of awe and appreciation, the state of mind that flows in grace. In surrendering to gravity, we give in to the fullness of all that we are.

*

Everyone has some resistance that we are holding on to. In the name of being right and making a point, we drift away from our fundamental intension of being happy. When we choose to let it go, despite our habit of resistance, we go with the flow of the authentic self. Joy requires releasing struggle, and then building a new reality based on this feeling of natural flow.

*

Either you are suffering from Miserable Bastard Syndrome, or enjoying Lucky Bastard Syndrome. It is all about which side of the equation you give your attention to.

*

We all find connection to skill. It is the embodiment of love in action. Anything we love, we eventually find skill within.

*

When you breathe deeply, and release your resistance, the way in which everything is going to be OK comes into view. You cannot see past how you feel. Seek better feelings, find better answers.

*

Often people believe that I suggest doing things that scare you despite your overwhelming fear. This is not exactly my point, and such a path can lead to some very bad outcomes. What I support is transforming how you feel about things that scare you, and then enjoying the expanded territory afforded by your new perspective.

*

You can try to punish yourself into success, but it is far more effective to enjoy the process of becoming, and grant yourself forgiveness for previous attempts that failed. Becoming is life, because life is about going somewhere, not about being somewhere.

*

Fear is motivation, like a whip from behind, while the joy of inspiration compels us forward out of the sheer pleasure of motion ahead. Genuine inspiration is pure life fuel, the only sustainable resource in the universe.

*

We often get confused in the epidemiology of success, thinking that the great feeling we have when we achieve success is caused by our attainment, when in fact the feeling is the cause of our success, every time, no exceptions.

*

Fear is our only resistance in life. When fear is gone, we are free to do what makes heart-sense to us. When we choose to ignore fear, we become ourselves in our unlimited form. Fear is very much like the drag felt by an aircraft in flight. The faster you fly, the more drag you will experience. It's not going away, so you might as well accept it.

*

Just as the child must bravely peek under their bed at night to see that there really are no monsters, we must clear our fear through exploring the truth of our concerns in rational probabilities, and then we must let the fear go once and for all. How else can we sleep in peace?

*

It is true that we are not born with much fear at all, but we learn it rather quickly. We learn through the example of others, negative experiences, and by fixating on what we don't want. We cannot blame the adults completely, because fear shows up anyway. The looping of thoughts that scare us is a natural cognitive behavior following an undesirable experience that is not easily forgotten. It can also become natural for us to transcend our fear through a deliberate focusing on the answers to our fear, and on thoughts that bring us relief. Anything that makes us feel better really is natural to a mind committed to happiness.

*

The source of human suffering is not about circumstances but our interpretation of circumstances. It is true that there are things of a profoundly unpleasant nature, but it is our continued attention to the downside of the situation that prevents us from focusing in a way that would make us happier; a way that ultimately leads to solutions to our fear. Safety is a product of a constructive imagination.

Mood is more than a symptom of circumstances; it is the mindset that leads to more circumstances similar to the way we are feeling. When we choose our direction of thought, we choose our mood, and when we choose our mood, we alter the path of our future.

*

Our bodies are more fragile than we realize, as we are susceptible to the effects of our physical environment. We must therefore take the time to clear ourselves of the past as a teacher cleans off the chalk from their clothes after school, and have the ability to begin again anew, over and over. If you do not allow the loving selfishness of a moment of grace, you have nothing to give anyone.

*

The skydivers trust each other. This is a consequence to having demonstrated bravery and competence. This is the very same unfolding that any team follows in the process of becoming a team. When we impress each other, we accept each other.

*

If you are not willing to look like a fool, you are not brave enough to be great.

*

If you are having a pity party, don't invite anyone. If you are having an appreciation party, invite the whole world.

*

The commitment to be as happy as possible is more important than anything else in life. There are plenty of reasons to have a bad day, and none of them will lead you where you want to go.

*

The sword of consciousness is best sharpened with focusing our attention on silence. Through contemplative action or peaceful inaction, we become comfortable with space, the place where infinite possibility is born.

*

It is no wonder that friendly aliens do not land on our planet and introduce themselves. We don't even want to sit next to the fat lady on the bus. How are going to handle a purple person? We must lean acceptance despite apparent differences, because in our core, we are one mind in many bodies.

*

Love matters more than being right. Rather being the sledgehammer of truth, reach for understanding and connection.

*

There are only two conversations, what we don't like, and the better possibilities that our repulsion leads us to realize. Depending on which conversation you engage in, you either become powerful and creative, or helpless and miserable.

Your choice...

*

There is a flawed premise about compassion that goes like this: "If someone is suffering, I must suffer too." This makes compassion look rather unappealing. In truth, we cannot starve ourselves enough to feed the hungry. In order to be of assistance, we must remain in our buoyant place of power, and call them lovingly toward where we are.

*

A man stood silently by a grave, listening to the stories told about the woman who had died. When the crowd departed, leaving only the clergyman, he softly spoke: "I loved that woman" he said, "and I almost told her once". The real cost of cowardice is regret.

*

The physical reality around you is merely a symptom of your past patterns of emotional fixation and beliefs. If you choose to conjure the feeling of how you want the future to be, you are always destined to live in happiness, creating what you desire. It all begins right here, right now. Visualization is creation.

*

No matter how bleak things may look, there is always a thought that turns the corner for you. The long list of things that you love are your best defense against that which brings you down. Look where you want to go.

*

There is plenty of evidence in both directions, so we might as well make our case that everything is going to work out fine. What we expect is what we get.

*

Clearly there is more to life than just keeping one's head above water. When we bring true happiness back to the table, everything works out better because matter is always subject to the intentions of consciousness. You are not on this Earth just to observe, you are here to create.

*

When a person chooses to cheer up, they make their own luck.

*

Belief without action accomplishes much more than action without belief. This is because when we allow our success to flow naturally, things coast toward where we want them to go with very little effort. When we allow our positive expectation, we are in a place of readiness to receive our success, like an open baseball glove waiting for the ball. When we doubt, we cannot take enough action to offset our disbelief in the possibility of things going the way we desire. Faith is the core element of all success.

*

Basking in the light of the glorious nature of existence, we realize that the basis of consciousness is joy.

*

Human suffering is just a brief sour note in a grand symphony of wellbeing.

*

Life can be scary, but with good breathing and a lively sense of humor, all things are possible.

*

Skill is safety, because life favors the competent.

Cooperation is more important than competence, because skill is not always enough.

*

An adventurous life is a beautiful life because in the pursuit of your personal version of happiness, you make the world a better place in a brand new way. When we celebrate in the joy of our transcended limitations, the whole of the Universe feels our emanation. Joy is non-local.

*

All that is required is continually profiting from your life's lessons and then giving your full attention to the creation of the best-case scenario that the worst case scenario has given birth to.

*

You are allowed to be afraid, you are just not allowed to let fear stop you from doing the right thing. Most often, the right thing is the scariest thing. Being afraid of being afraid mutes out light and limits our possibilities. Accept the fear and let is flow through you, it is not who you are, just what you feel when you take your eyes off the road. Train your eyes on the spaces between obstacles, and the fear will be limited to a surge of excitement that is merely voluntary entertainment.

*

The ability to find fault is most often incompatible with happiness and harmony. What we look for is what we find.

*

Your untapped potential is only limited by your ability to envision a better set of possibilities. Think grand, be grand.

\*

Going with the flow of happiness means going with the flow of wellbeing in all its forms. Resisting happiness, regardless of the reason, means resisting wellbeing in all its forms.

\*

Cultivation of the ability to focus on the wanted that the unwanted has clarified is the only game in town.

\*

Slow down into your personal version of beauty.

\*

There are lots of opportunities for you to experience your own personal version of fear. If you face your fear too directly, you are in for a traumatic experience, and consequently your fear will get worse. If, on the other hand, you take a gentler, slower approach, you will make headway. For every inch you move toward expanding beyond your fears, you make quantum leaps in your journey toward freedom and happiness. Fear is always an opportunity for expansion.

\*

Deciding to interpret the events before you as leading toward improvement is what makes it so.

*

Landing your parachute where you want to is a
consequence of believing in your parachute, and in yourself.
It is a synergy of nylon, flesh, understanding and intention.
Believing in yourself is a natural consequence of knowing
who you are.

*

If you do not trust yourself, you cannot love yourself. If you
cannot love yourself, no one else can trust you.

When you feel doubt in yourself, state aloud: "I am Aware. I
am Competent. I am Trustworthy." Words are spells within
our minds, and they are heard by the Universe. Command
your power.

*

Inner freedom comes as a result of shedding both our
preconceived limitations and our fears of what will happen
when we do.

*

There is no such thing as limitation, only failure to challenge
the perceived boundaries of our consciousness.

*

The only fear worth harboring is the fear of living without true passion.

*

Fearlessness is not the same thing as being without a clear knowledge of the risks. Fear paralyzes, caution respects.

*

No matter how horrible the object of attention, there is always an aspect that creates an improvement that would not have happened otherwise. Be thankful for all that is.

*

All that we do is in the pursuit of a better feeling. In order to achieve this, however, the often-disregarded requirement is to be in the mood of positive expectation when the opportunity arises. We can only live what is already within us.

*

The fear of dying can sometimes lead to survival, but only if we follow it to the joy of skill.

*

Fear is not always the cause of danger, but focus on those possibilities certainly increases the odds of things going badly. Glimpsing in the direction that you don't want to go is not the same thing as fixating your way into an unpleasant ordeal.

*

Relaxing into focusing on the details of making your dreams come true truly scary stuff. Without breaching that fear, we do not take the baby steps that move us in the right direction. Without action, there is no material experience. One step, and then the next.

Believing that you have money in your future is the first step away from poverty. One who has hope is never completely poor. Living the experience of sustainable abundance requires first the belief, then inspired action, combined with an authentic sense of worthiness that allows the experience to flow. If you don't believe you deserve it, you will be the wrench in your gears.

*

The wave of wellbeing caries us only as far as our worthiness allows.. Notice the programs you have been looping in your mind that have made you feel shame, and face them head-on. Look these thoughts straight in the eyes and say: "I do not believe in you anymore. You are a lie." If you define yourself as your higher self, and there is no limit to how good life can be.

*

A fearless approach to challenge may not be the only way ahead, but it is the only one that goes the whole distance. Sustainable success requires total commitment in mind, body and spirit.

*

Melancholy and lethargy go hand in hand with a fear-based frame of mind because when there is no hope, there is no life energy. The heart of fearlessness comes from the joy of absolute focus on the dream of more, better, more, better. From the place of power called joy, all life force energy flows.

*

Holding your happiness for ransom to motivate is a self-defeating mindset. You can feel joy in every step if you allow it. Most of our journey is the freefall between steps, so we might as well enjoy the ride.

*

The appreciation we will enjoy in our positive future is created by the comparison to our negative past. Remembering this as the negative present is raging is what starts the process of appreciation right here right now. Eventually, you will look back on all of it and see its value. Might as well begin now.

*

We are not here to tell the story of what is, we are here to make it better. We do this by transcending the complaint mentality, and graduating to the expansion mentality. How can things get better if you don't wonder how?

*

Slow down. This is not a race.

Slow is grace, and grace is beauty.

*

Skill is simply good planning and great breathing resulting in graceful flowing action. This combination gets us where we want to go. Incompetence is poor planning and bad breathing resulting in chaos that makes us want to plan and breathe better next time.

*

When you are pissed off and you just vent, you are wasting your energy and fueling the feeling of helplessness. When you are pissed off and you act with the expectation that your efforts will improve the situation, you are a powerful creator in touch with your emotions. Turn in the direction of the solution, not back toward the problem.

*

The alternative to brave love is cowardly regret. Tell them before you lose them.

175

*

Best not to use your high standards as your excuse to ignore the little miracles all around you. Happiness is selective perception.

*

You are more than you see when you are down. You are even more than you see when you are up. You are nothing less than the full expression of all that you desire, never-endingly expanding toward the possibility of better.

*

Challenges are always opportunities when we learn from what we have lived, and move forward into the better possibilities clarified by our difficulties. Better is created by worse.

*

Although we always believe that we are able envision the best possibility, there is always more. Reach beyond the given toward the expansion of better.

*

When you are in a good mood: first thought, best thought. When you are in a lousy mood: first thought, worst thought. Don't automatically believe everything you think.

*

Complaint is just celebration looking in the opposite direction. When you know what you don't want, you know what you want instead.

*

The ability to observe and report is nothing without the ability to look for elements of the desired. Seek and ye shall find.

*

Fantasy is reality in the baking. Dream big.

*

Something just changed. Something shifted. Something loosened and let more light in. It is all going to get better now. Are you ready?

*

Fear is always proportional to our level of love. The more we love, the more we fear losing what we love. Nevertheless, pure love is always a consequence of focusing on aspects of appreciation, and has nothing to do with fear at all.

*

Do not let your plans distract you from what the universe has planned for you.

*

The universe continues to exist because there is always room for improvement. Enjoying "what is" creates the expansion of "even better than this".

*

Love is a verb; either you are doing it or you are not.

*

Although blaming others always feels better than despair, self-blame has more opportunity for inspired improvement.

*

Just as your favorite food is something you may have not yet tried, your personal best has yet to come.

*

"What if this goes badly?" is an important question, but not nearly as important as: "What if this goes really, really well?".

*

Unhappiness is the consequence of the belief that happiness is contingent upon things going right.

*

Your next breath has the potential to be the most refreshing
of your entire life.

*

To trust or not to trust, this is the question.

*

Believing in one another is humanity's most dangerous, and
most necessary step of all.

*

Love is who we are. Anything else is just another name for
neurosis.

*

Positive emotion is the core feeling of all sanity.

*

Nurturing the mood that we prefer is the only way to create
the future that we prefer.

*

This moment is the doorway, this breath is the key.

*

The only sustainable happiness is the kind that comes wrapped in self-assigned worthiness. Ya gotta dig you.

*

When we are finding flaws in others, we are not squelching the incompetence, we are magnifying it. Praising what we love is the best way to get more of it and everything like it.

*

When leaders make choices based on what is least scary, things get really scary. Brave choices are always necessary for good leadership.

*

Why is it that cranky people always believe that being right justifies being nasty? Right or not, we need to be nicer to each other or this whole thing is a wash.

*

Long-term loving relationships are a symptom of a lousy memory and a good imagination. We must look for what we are wanting to see in our beloved, and forgive previous attempts at kindness that feel short. Don't define them as their lowest moments, know them by their most loving moments. This perspective not only magnifies your affection, but is the cause of a refreshed love of the world.

*

Deciding that the people around you need to act differently in order for you to be happy takes all of your power to smile anytime you want to and gives it to them.

In other words, when we demand others to change, and we say that we are going to be pissed I they don't do what we prefer, the cost is too high. Your joy is not leverage, and it is non-negotiable.

*

Controlling the flow of consciousness within another sentient being is an impossible task. Better to make your happiness, or unhappiness entirely your fault, and take them off the hook. Free them, free you.

*

The best way to return the world of humanity to the balance of nature is to open a door, walk out into creation, and breathe in the wellbeing. The balance of nature was within us all along.

*

Complaining without hope of improvement is what happens when we focus on what is, rather than what we prefer instead. This way of focusing holds us in a place of dissatisfaction until we change our story for the better.

*

Telling it like it is just holds us where we are by bringing more of the same into our lives. Telling it like we want it to be leads us toward a rendezvous with the improvement we have been asking for. The low hanging fruit of the better world still requires someone tall enough to pick it.

*

When I am ready, things will go the way I want them to go, but often I believe I need to vent and complain and justify why I need the improvement, which is exactly what holds me apart from the improvement that I desire.

You've got to cheer up into the improvement that is waiting for you.

*

The dream of tomorrow has no pull unless it is savored in the now. This moment is all there is.

*

Silence plus nature equals wellbeing.

*

The people misspeaking in the name of religion would have turned the planet completely upside down by now, far worse than they have, were it not for the sane majority from within the religious structures. Organizations are made up of people with mostly common ideals, and at the core of each of these is compassionate sanity. Don't get me wrong, I am not against religion at all. I am, however, against those who use it as an excuse to wage separation, hatred and war. The pursuit of the Divine sometimes leads to love, but the pursuit of love always leads to the Divine.

*

There have been atrocities committed in the name of every spiritual tradition and ideology that humans hold dear. We must not over-simplify the situation. Vilifying has never created lasting peace. We can always find reasons to declare war, perhaps we should be looking for the reasons to declare peace.

*

Fear not for our future, love is always there.

*

The pursuit of fearlessness amidst very real reasons to fear is the path that leads us to both our best nature, and to each other.

*

We must take on adventures of all kinds, in which success is richly rewarded and failure equally weighted toward the opposite experience. Risk is a direct reflection of the magnitude of the danger, which always forces our attention into the present moment. Danger creates enlightenment.

*

The world is full of people who have succeeded in not dying. A rarer sort are those who chose meaningful risk and walk away with meaningful rewards.

*

The world has always belonged to the brave.

*

Be your own personal hero.

*

Life is not about being dealt a perfect hand; it is about making this one work too.

*

The fear of change is what prevents most improvement in this world. Without the risk of worse, there is no better.

*

If you aren't thrilled about the old, you cannot allow yourself to fear the new.

*

Justification, vilification and objectification are the means we give for waging war. Appreciation, compassion and mutual respect are the means by which we create peace. Both are deliberate delusions, but only one of them leads to the experience that the Universe desires for us.

*

It is easier to blame than it is to take responsibility. Being a blame-thrower burns up the possibility of being a light-shiner. It isn't about who is wrong, it is about what is right.

*

It is the enforcement of objective principles that leads to most of the cruelty in the world. Kindness matters more than righteousness. Cold enforcement of the letter of the law most often results in a loss of the spirit of the law, which is intended to nurture wellbeing and harmony. Grace is the intelligence to know when to ignore rules and expectations, and put humanity first.

*

New may bring danger, but old without thought is far more insidious.

*

Mood is not about external reality, it is about internal reality, caused by the way we interpret external reality through our beliefs. We are always free to be happy because we are always free to choose our beliefs.

*

Freaking out is just a sign that you actually give a shit. If you want to create a desirable outcome, you must not freak out but chill out, and focus on taking steps to make that happen. Caring for the world includes caring how you feel about the world. When you are freaking out, you are putting more faith in lack and powerlessness than you are abundance and your ability to produce it. Care enough to fix your mood so that your give-a-shit can be effective.

*

Brilliance is always obscured by fear, and revealed through the choice to go with authentic inspiration over safety.

*

I am starting to see now that fear is less about adrenalin and more about avoidance. When we steer a wide birth around a subject or experience, fear is replacing freedom with limitation. Happiness requires "chutzpah" (loosely translated from Yiddish: guts).

*

Who you fearlessly dreamed you were as a child is who you really are. Our true nature is the high mark of our imagination. Dare to awaken to the dreams of your inner child.

*

The reason it feels so lousy when you act out of fear is because your true self is fearless. Be you or be disappointed.

*

If you are too lazy or afraid to send good vibes to random strangers through warm eye contact, you are part of the problem. It feels so much better to be part of the solution. Love everyone, everywhere, all the time.

*

The self-imposed limits we create today are the barriers we will have to transcend tomorrow. Limitation is just an opportunity for expansion.

*

The simple act of complaining in order to fill a space in conversation is the slippery slope that leads to a miserable day. Appreciation is the only doorway to lasting happiness.

*

Freedom is not free. The price we must pay is the forfeiture of laziness. It disguises itself as comfort, but fear by any other name is still fear.

*

Fortune favors the optimistic, since all things are fortunate to those who look for the silver lining.

*

Everything, pleasurable and painful, clarifies preference. This means that it all really is good. It all leads to wisdom.

*

Our differences do not separate us, they are our common bond. In our diversity, we are beautiful.

*

Striving to be normal at the expense of our true nature is how the mundane middle eclipses the beautiful extremes. Weird is wonderful.

*

It is the silencing of those of appropriate anger for the convenience of the greater good that robs the world of both truth and justice. Harmony is not loving when it becomes compliance to unloving ways. Do not rage against the aspects of our world that require change, but do not be silent. Sometimes waves in the other direction are needed to reverse an unloving flow.

*

When we let it move freely through us, it is perfectly clear that love really is what makes the world go around. Our resilience is assured when we feel our connection to love's power, because we have hung our sails high in the wind that moves the Universe.

*

There are only two kinds of people in a crisis. Those who soothe their fear with constructive thought and action, and those who make it hard for them to get things done.

*

Without confronting our fear of silence, we cannot effectively overcome any other fear. Changing gears from reverse to forward always requires a little time in neutral.

*

This is a brand new day. The degree to which things can be improved should not be underestimated.

*

It may seem appropriate to be pissed off or deeply saddened about something, but the feeling is a far cry from a solution. Prolonged justifiable anger is just pacing in an unlocked cage, expecting no escape. Emotional buoyancy leads to freedom from all that brings us down.

*

Sometimes you need to forget who you are in order to remember who you want to be.

*

Justifying why we can't is how we pave the way to failure. Invest in the visualization of where you want to go, not the possibility of where you don't. You will live in the possibility that you think about most, so think wisely.

*

Dare to trust yourself enough to risk your ass to save your soul.

*

Without fearlessly acting upon what we know is right, we lose the power that comes along with knowing that we are on the right side of the fence. Fear and laziness simply cost too much.

*

The beauty of fear is the way it brings about a deep appreciation for what we love when we briefly think that we are going to lose it forever. The beauty of love is that it lasts forever, even when we fear that it doesn't.

*

True freedom is not the opposite of bondage, but the relief from perceived limits within us.

*

Realizing that you are more than you have been is the first step toward shedding your fear of the future. Embrace your expansion, and stand in the gloriousness of who you are.

*

What if your fear has been the only thing preventing the expression of your amazing true nature? What if you chose, in this moment, to let it go? What if you undermined with lies that fear has told you with the truth. You are much more than you have demonstrated thus far. Know who you are, and the rest is easy.

*

What would the political arena be like without the fear of change and the fear of truth?

*

Where the light shines, the darkness recedes. The darker the dark gets, the brighter the bright looks. Fear does not retreat from love; it dissolves into it. The darkness becomes a new kind of light, informed by the human experience, more savvy to the ways of the world. Love, when made specific, shifts from being a noun to being a verb, kinetic in its expression. This is the reason for the Universe, the illusion of separation. We are here to be love in form, ignoring the illusions, carrying out a brand new way to shine.

*

Justifying the need for improvement is not the same thing as clarifying what the improvement will be. Are you envisioning or complaining?

*

Patience and bravery are born in the same place. A deep breath gives rise to a new focus of attention that leads us where we want to go, and suddenly everything changes.

*

We can push back our fear if we want to. Remember, it is not about shedding fear entirely, but stepping beyond your personal comfort zone, little by little. If you manage to put your toes in the surf today, perhaps tomorrow you will get in up to your knees. One step at a time, you go further, and grow larger. Remember why, and the how will come into form. Expansion, expansion, expansion.

*

Have love for yourself as you walk slowly through your perceived limitations, and watch your world expand.

*

Be light about all of this. If it isn't fun, you are just moving too fast. Slow down but don't stop. Argue for your freedom, and then prove yourself right. This is how we move beyond the illusions in our minds, the untruths that we formerly accepted as real.

*

I love how adventure challenges cause me to either rise to the occasion or die a horrible death. Hero, or zero. I must plan and prepare before launching out of safe harbors, and as I do so, I learn valuable life lessons that apply to everything else in my life. The challenges show me who I am. Therefore, excessive safety is profoundly dangerous.

*

I find it interesting that what I truly appreciate was once something that I desired but did not have. It would seem that being on the way to things that I desire is something to be appreciated as well. This realization brings a new appreciation for our unmanifested desires. May it help us all to graduate from the incessant complaining that we have not yet achieved our goals, so that we can focus intently on the feeling and steps that make our dreams come true. In the taking of these steps, we must reside in the feeling of eagerness and movement towards our goal. We are already living in our dream, knowing that the birthing process is unfolding.

*

"That is the way we've always done it" is the mindset that fear and overwhelment lead toward. When we believe that we cannot endure any more pain, whether it be the pain of fear and anger, or the physical exhaustion that follows along with doing things the hard way, this is when we stop living and start dying. Unless we are expanding with passion, into challenge and danger, we are cut off from the life force that animates us. Ultimately it is our love of life that gives us lift. This attitude is sometimes brought forth through joyful experiences, but it is also spurred by experiences of prolonged suffering providing the contrast that yields appreciation for relief.

*

Love is the place that we come from and the place we are destined to return. Happiness is nothing if it does not lead to compassion, appreciation and grateful effort. Love is authentic life force in the driver's seat, the real you taking the helm. Things always lead to better when we find our way to joy. If we could maintain that indefinitely, there would be no need for uplifting books, music or inspirational experience. Apparently, despite our best intentions, we will fall from joy. The meaning of separation from bliss is the experience of regaining it. It is not just about being in the Garden, it is about returning to the Garden.

*

It is not always your fault, but most of the time it is our mood that leads to our speed that leads to us missing a turn in life and wishing we hadn't. We zig when we should have zagged, and we get a painful lesson. Some of those lessons sting for a long time, but if there is one truth that governs the Universe that we live in, it is change. Although some things take time to change, all things are impermanent, including happiness. Fortunately, what we desire has a way of returning. We may not always change the now that much, but we can have a massive effect on the future. Our suffering leads us to knowing what we do not want to do again, and helps us envision the opposite. Our experience, joyful or painful, provides priceless information for the journey toward sustainable happiness and the wisdom to attain it.

*

The new is always dangerous, but without that risk, nothing will ever get any better than this. Take a chance when it feels right to your bones, and never look back in fear. This life if yours for the making.

*

There is a great deal of improvement that you are calling forth with your desire, and all of what you are asking for is

195

being assembled as we speak. In the meantime, soften yourself. Relax into knowing that everything is alright, and will be even better. I understand that it can be hard to see the light when others in your life seem to be committed to being miserable and want to spread their misery to you. Nevertheless, requiring others to change in any way in order to please you is always a losing battle because you can never control them. All you can do is control your own focus of attention and the thoughts that you choose to indulge

*

You cannot directly change the people in your life, but you can have influence. Free will prevents the possibility of assertion of your will on another being. You can however, stand as a shining example of positive focus and appreciation, and guide others with your life as a demonstration of what is possible. Even if what they observe in you is way beyond where they are at the time, they will eventually see the merit of your attitude. Everyone desires happiness, and even when we seem to be determined to be unhappy, the underlying human desire for joy continues to be a plan looking for a way to unfold. Let them see.

*

You were born being of pure light. You are a teacher and a healer and a lover and an uplifter. When you walk that path, you will feel wonderful. Guaranteed. When you use anything as your excuse to live a more selfish and unhappy way, you are not being you. The negative emotion that you inevitably feel is your indication that you are off track. Your gut is your guide when you realize that the path of the real you is the way to everything you want and need. Quite simply, being the most inspired version of you is the only option if you are to be happy.

*

It is easy to feel overwhelmed by the heaviness of your responsibility to be the ever-expanding potential that lies ahead. Remember that the story of your life is a tiny aspect of the massive you that is a constantly evolving soul, reaching for more. This is just one moment of many, and the tip of a very large iceberg. Your decision to serve the highest good within yourself and above yourself is all you need to stay on course. Even when you have lost hope, the realization of your true nature is always there to rediscover.

*

The real you never disappears; it just hides behind the plot that is playing out. The role that you are playing is partly free will in action, and partly the continuation of a storyline that you only partly set in motion. The job at hand is not an easy one. If anyone tells you otherwise you can follow them until life proves them wrong. Life is both beautiful and ugly, joyful and horrible, passionate and infuriating. This show is real. On the other hand, our free will remains. We are free to interpret our role in the plot as one that has wiggle room for interpretation and freedom to maneuver.

*

Life is school. You can either be a good student and realize the moral of the story, or take lots and lots of painful lessons over an over until you get the message.

*

As you take on the unbelievable challenge that happiness and expansion require, go easy. Breathe deep, and know that you are supported from every direction. Detach yourself from the exquisite drama that you signed up for in order to allow the optimism that creates further expansion. Enjoy the thrill of being alive: simple, peaceful, loving and appreciative of the value of the journey.

*

This is fine, whatever it is. The thing you have been worrying about is probably not as horrible as your first-glance reaction.  Remember that even the bad stuff leads to a beautiful new kind of improvement. The human heart, and the ingenious nature of the human mind, has no limit. Our humanness is not about our inconsistency. Our creativity is the source of both folly and brilliance, because it is by definition, unpredictable. Our humanity is the source of our lovability as a species. If there is any reason for Mother Earth to keep us around, it is our insight and love that we show when purpose and appreciation win over fear and anger. Perhaps that is why she lets us exist despite our short-sighted technology. That will change too. In the meantime, we must demonstrate our true value and grow above and beyond the machines that we have created, things that make our lives both easier and more complicated. Nature is simple and graceful and cooperative. When we strive to become more like nature, we experience harmony in our lives. When we apply our brilliant creativity to nature's ways, we do what we came to do: to make the world a better place.

*

It is dangerous to be completely open and kind, but it is also dangerous to be cold and selfish. Choose your stunt.

*

We are imperfect. Our path is imperfect. We are going to succeed, and we are going to fail. If we keep moving forward. we will continue to fail our way to magnificence. We must appreciate the roller coaster of life for its gifts of wisdom.  Without down, there is no up.

*

The flame of insight is always eager to grow, given adequate oxygen. Breathe Big, Dream Big.

*

The ability to recognize the necessity of a reduction in situational speed is the ultimate demonstration of intelligence.

*

Speed combined with inadequate respiration results in a contracted mindset that reduces the likelihood of grace and genius.

*

Profound failures begin and often end with a failure to breathe.

Peace begins right here; there's no place like Om.

*

It is one thing to be loved, it is another to let it in.

*

When there is fear, there is no power. When there is power, there is no fear.

*

YOU ARE DOING YOGA RIGHT NOW

Whatever you are doing, do it better.

Do it with grace.

Do it with better breathing.

Do it with clarity of intention, and smoothness of action.

*DO IT WITH LOVE.*

\*

The speed and complexity of our world has led us to treat others as objects rather than real people. It is time to slow down and see everyone we encounter as deep characters, with real stories, worthy of our love and respect.

They are all just you, in their shoes.

\*

Let your fear be replaced by faith in yourself, and in the magic that holds this universe together.

\*

True power is not demonstrated through force, but through the influence of intelligent love.

\*

Outer peace begins with inner peace, and inner peace comes from burying the hatchet of anger and resentment and daring to fall in love with humanity all over again.

*

The global warming I am interested in is caused by smiles, not fossil fuels. Your kind eyes are more powerful than you can see.

*

Transcending is the process of going through, not around the emotion. When one transcends fear, they first realize the cause for this fear, and notice its effects, still remembering who they are. Choose to look beyond the danger to come into alignment with the heroic version of yourself. Fear places its faith in chaos and lack of power, and it makes your small. A mind focused on courage experiences the thoughts and sensations of fear, but chooses to bravely rise through it and beyond it. Know who you are, and there is no need for fear. You are a survivor.

*

We must not confuse what is for what can be.

*

Forward eventually leads upward.

*

Spiritually focused people have traditionally avoided struggle and strife in favor of inner peace, and thus evaded many unpleasant subjects such as politics as a result. It is those who are most morally and spiritually advanced who must stand up and speak loudly now. Without love-minded people bravely speaking their minds, politics inevitably backslides into immorality and corruption. Speak love into being.

*

OCCUPY THE HEART.

*

Honesty without compassion is brutality. Don't be the sledgehammer of truth. Be skillful means by which truth proliferates.

*

Without the dangerous pursuit of truth, there is no freedom. Let us speak it with love for all, vilifying no person, and instead focus on solutions rather than crucifixions. Punishment however justified is not progress, as it always leads away from the loving-kindness that is at the heart of any morally based movement in the world.

*

Sustainable freedom requires fearless love of human rights, and the willingness to speak truth to power despite the risks. Speak truth with loving ways, and stand up for humanity without putting others down. Forgive them for they knew not that they knew not.

*

Freedom must be bravely claimed by those who remember its true value, or it will be taken away by those who value power and money over liberty and equality. With absolute adherence to the principles of non-violence, the loving and caring must wage a war of principles against the absence of compassion. We must resist bondage by occupying freedom and living in love.

*

The deep breath that ushers in the feeling of grace is the beginning of the new world.

*

The lesson our generation is learning is that we need far less stuff than we have had, and far more compassionate loving-kindness than we dreamed possible.

*

As we continue down the path toward civil justice, the desire for improvement often leads us to feel anger towards injustice. We must remember that moral goals will never be achieved through immoral means. We will improve our world through love, and love alone.

*

Being happy isn't the only thing to do, it's just the most fun thing to do, which almost always leads to even better. Good moves in the direction of Great, which is why happy people are more likely to succeed in life. Love Matters.

*

Being fortunate without basking in appreciation is a waste of good fortune. Thankfulness is the doorway to perpetual joy.

*

Both peace and love require trust. Trust requires deliberate ignorance of erroneous evidence pointing toward mistrust. We look for what we want to see, and so we create a place for it to exist.

*

A society's relationship to fear and risk is what determines its overall success. A brave culture that strives for all that is right and just will not cower at the consequences to this commitment, and instead will focus its attention on the sole prospect of reaching for something better. Truth feels better than falsehood, making it easy to spot. What is true is that all beings are worthy and equal in the eyes of the Universe. This truth is the basis for a moral and just society. This is a risky idea to deploy, in the context of the belief in good and evil. It is uncomfortable and dangerous for our old mindset to consider the value of someone committed to doing harm. Nevertheless, if justice is to be moral, we must treat others with respect, even those we call criminals. They have allowed their minds to get off track, and they have done wrong, but that does not make them less than human. They are just misguided. Penal facilities must not be concentration camps to carry out our vengeance, but instead can be rehabilitation centers, operated with loving intention. Protecting the innocent need not cause pollution of our own karma as a people. All are holy beings worthy of love. If we are to ascend into love as a society, we must uncover all of the unloving ways that once separated us from what love desires for our world. Everything is either love or a call to love. No exceptions.

*

Being right never gave anyone the authority to be cruel or disrespectful. Right or wrong, we must remember that vibe is the most important aspect of our interactions. The core principle of sustainable civilization is loving-kindness. Speak your truth with love.

*

The very same wind that carries us through the sky and across oceans is what returns us to a state of grace and flow when we welcome it deeply into our bodies.

*

Thankfulness is how we say yes to more love and happiness.

*

True heroes are not without fear. They know the consequences to failure, but choose to focus on the rewards of a meaningful life, and the exhilarating journey that leads there.

*

Passing on good vibes when you have them is the most valuable thing anyone can do for society.

*

Positive emotion is the source of every good idea you will ever have. It is your indication that the real you agrees with the right now you.

\*

Going with the flow of positive emotion is the wisest thing any of us will ever do. Joy is wisdom.

\*

Passive resistance is often misinterpreted to mean catatonic ignorance of unacceptable circumstances. Nothing could be further from the truth. Effective non-violent resistance is inspired truth in action: The heart filled with love raging against all that is not love, gently.

\*

The best part of an argument is making up and remembering that we love each other. It's not about the issue, it is about the desire for connection that wasn't being served.

\*

When we decide that love is our way, even when the mongers rattle their sabers and pound their drums, nobody will show up. Let hate die on the vine, unpicked.

\*

Our world is far from perfect, and it is the brave who will move what has been into what will be. When bravery goes beyond the hearts of heroes and enters the realm of the common person, we will realize our destiny as a society driven by loving-kindness. Peace is not out there, it is with you.

*

Appreciating diversity is the way we stitch together the quilt of humanity. Together in our differences, we are beautiful.

*

Breathe big, think big, and take care of each other. Love leads to survival.

*

The skydivers all seem to have come to the conclusion that finding a way to remain calm and have fun seems to be best way to stay alive. When we make our mood our first priority, our positive attitude leads to both skill and safety. Enjoy the harrowing journey.

*

What if you were right when, in your good mood, you pronounced that everything was going to be alight?

It's true.

Let that in.

*

My message to humanity, a prayer for fearlessness: Sing songs in the darkness. The Light of Love prevails. Gather now together, heal yourselves.

*

Vibe is pivotal. Choose your mood, create your world.

*

Freedom: My thoughts, my choice.

*

There are always more answers than we can see from where we stand. Keep moving, shifting and changing, and the light will come into view.

*

Most of life's answers to scary problems are found in coordinating and harmonizing with others, but we instead often miss seeing the solutions because we are too busy stewing, complaining and justifying our anger. The "ME" generation died alone and miserable; it is time for the "US" generation.

There are many valid reasons to feel negative emotion, but not one of them is worth focusing on for more than fifteen seconds. If you can resolve the issue in that amount of time, great. If not, get off the topic before you make a habit of the emotion. People steeped in negative emotion are not all that much fun to be around, even when they are right.

*

Demonstrations in the street have started the ball of change rolling toward the possibilities of improvement. Now we must remember that without love, a fearless demonstration quickly becomes a riot. We must love the protesters, and the police, and join together to evolve this movement from "angry complaint" into an experience of "compassionate unification". We are ONE.

*

Fear most often leads to irrationality. The more adverse the possibility, the more we tend to overestimate the likelihood of it occurring. This is the reason why much of the human race steers such a wide birth around risk, at the expense of the possible rewards. We mistake the magnitude of our emotion for the likelihood of actualization. Ironically, though self-fulfilling prophesies of failure, we usually prove ourselves right. Fear makes danger real.

*

Open the doors to the real you that you have been too afraid to divulge for fear of judgment. Only you decide your worthiness. Only you can let it in. Don't judge them, and stop judging you. Just be yourself, in all your majestic glory, warts and all.

*

Heart opening realizations are the beginning of humanity's healing process, but positive thoughts must lead us to constructive action. Thinking nice is the start, being nice is the way.

*

Wellness requires exercise. Exercise hurts. Only the brave will choose to do what they know will hurt. Therefore, the pursuit of wellness is always braver than laziness.

*

Fearlessness Meditation:

My eyes are open. My heart is open. My hands are open. My ears are open. My voice is sweet. My mind is soft. My love is shining, shining, shining. I am strong. Let me serve.

*

Reasonable precautions are part of an effective fear-abatement approach. Check our parachute. Any worry that cannot be addressed with action is just neurosis, and must be addressed internally with improved breathing and faith in the hospitable nature of the universe. Once the checks are complete, surrender to trust.

*

Fear is contended with in two ways. The first is through an internal soothing process, and the second is through addressing the external conditions. If you are worried about a parachute malfunction, pack your parachute well. Reasonable steps toward safety make it easier to feel better about danger. In the end, however, relief is always a choice to relax into feeling better.

*

If you are worried about the cold winter, get a coat, create an alternate heat source for your home, get blankets, and backup food and water. Then, make sure everyone around you has enough as well. We contend with danger side by side. Together we are a copious Potluck Supper, but alone we are toast, with no butter. Being prepared is not paranoia, it is prudence. Do it with grace and joy and not fear. Love the fact that you are using your brain to save your skin, and help all you can. That's what love does.

*

Sustainable peace requires us to extinguish all of our inner wars, and regain a heart of love for all people regardless of their differences. We may not agree with every choice they make, but we can still appreciate them for who and what they really are. Fearless love transcends all distinctions, colors and flags. Love everyone, because they are a part of you.

*

There are no walking stereotypes; there are only real people. In an attempt to simplify our surroundings we objectify people, ignoring their distinctiveness. Seeing the beautiful complexity within each person is how we transcend the trap of oversimplification and awaken our compassion for humanity.

*

Feeding the hungry, clothing the cold, cheering up the hopeless; this is how humanity walks the path of heroism, the way of love. Kindness is the basis of civilization.

*

Have you smiled at a stranger today? World peace begins in your eyes.

*

Worry is fixation of what we fear, just as joy is fixation in the other direction. When you are stuck in worry, forgive yourself and fixate on silence and peace. It is a place in your mind. Then, as you begin to feel relief, start reading from the Book of Joy, the aspects of your life experience that bring light to your mind. If you don't take the time to read it, you will inevitably start reading from the Book of Woes.

*

Although there may be similarities, today is not yesterday. The now is wide open. Are you picturing the best-case scenario, or just more of yesterday?

*

When the worst-case scenario hits, we awaken compassion. In striving to be of assistance, we see each other. We begin to recognize the depth and beauty of the people we otherwise would have passed quick judgment upon and dismissed as irrelevant. Worse yet, we may have seen them as obstacles to our wellbeing, as competition to be defeated. When we are in peril, we become beautiful because we are forced into harmony. We let go of our fear and reach for each other because we realize that we need each other.

*

If we are to breathe more sanity into our society, we must take the brave step of fearless cooperation in between disasters as well. By consciously choosing to see the depth and complexity within each person we cross paths with, and look for the beauty within them, and we will find it. In doing so, we will warm the melting pot of magnificent diversity that our world has become.

*

The ability to logically assess risk is the skill that diminishes the most when we allow fear to take root. We feel fear because we are fixating on the negative possibilities, and we consequently skew our expectations toward the unlikely negative possibilities. We must therefore always give the majority of our attention to the likely best-case scenario, because things almost always go down that road when we visualize and expect wellbeing. You aren't just observing the world, you are creating it.

*

Heroes are not made, they are born. We are all born to go big. It is true that in executing a legendary neighborhood stunt does bring you up a notch in the eyes of your mates, but more importantly, when you fly your bicycle over 14 garbage cans and land it, you feel differently about yourself. I know I certainly did. As we execute deliberate, well-thought-out stunts in life, both physical and emotional, we expand into the heroic nature that is our true essence. Through confirming demonstrations of our heroism on the outside, we remember who we really are on the inside.

*

As we live our lives, we are constantly jumping through metaphorical flaming hoops. We make a choice to take one step toward danger, and we are forced by circumstances to perform brilliantly in one way or another. When we are feeling good, and going with the flow, we skillfully demonstrate what is possible when someone does that particular thing the right way. We shine. This is a demonstration of the inner valor inherent in the human spirit.

*

Worthiness is a glow about a person that happens when self-esteem flows through them. This occurs due to a ritual that earns our own respect. When you do something unequivocal, that breaks the old mold of self-image to make room for a larger one, you have performed a stunt. You have expanded your sense of worthiness. Once we accept our worthiness without question, rituals are no longer necessary, and we can just be it.

*

When we sprinkle our problem in a glass full of hope, we create a solution that makes the problem disappear.

*

One happy solution-oriented person is more powerful than a thousand miserable complainers.

*

If someone calls you a child, the ego's response is one of offense. This is a bizarre distortion, because if you really think about it, there is no greater compliment. Our minds are clear and full of love when we are children, and if we allow it, we can be that again. We are just children, later.

*

When you are still screaming "no" at the problem, you are not emotionally congruent with the solution. If you desire wealth, you cannot feel impoverished. If you desire justice, you cannot get there through your anger about injustice. If you desire peace, you must have peace in your heart.

\*

The perfect world is in the making, as we observe the interactions of the world as it is, and dream of better. The more we dream, the easier it will be for us to join together and move gracefully into the benevolence and kindness that is natural to us. As we fearlessly look forward to what is on the way, the selfish ways of today will simply become a tale from the past that created our new future. We will lay down our weapons of greed and lust and anger, and band together in mutual caring. Be assured, love will prevail.

\*

Anger only helps us lift off from fear and hopelessness. Once we are airborne, however, we must lift our eyes and our hearts from anger and reach for a feeling of hope if we are to get to the improvement we desire. Clinging to negative emotion always brings us back down, even when it is our reason for taking flight.

\*

Finding fault is how we expand into improvement. Dwelling on fault is how we become a miserable person that nobody wants to be around. It is a matter of time management. If your conversations occasionally touch on solutions but return to orbit around the problem, you are a complainer. If you spend just a few moments talking about the problem, and the rest of your conversation talking about the solution, you are a creator.

*

You can't smell the flowers when you are speeding down the highway at 80. Slow down to the speed of nature, and the beauty of life reveals itself.

*

The core principle of homeopathic medicine is to treat unwanted conditions with a tiny bit of the condition itself. Worded differently, homeopathy gives you the symptoms of what you are striving to alleviate, so that your body's natural homeostasis can return the balance that is inherent in all living organisms. This is exactly why adventure-provoked fear can, and usually does help us reduce our ambient stress level. We must step into fear in order to cultivate the skill of courage.

*

Being a positive person is not about avoiding the negative but instead learning from it, and then letting it go.

*

When the ambient stress level is maintained at a high level for a long period of time, we look for any excuse at all to run and hide, reaching for physiological balance. Rest is part of strength. Although the motive may be a much-needed feeling of relief, the bottom line is, stress causes laziness. We go and we stop, and then we go again; it is all part of the experience. Attachment to laziness is simply addiction to methods of rest that are unrestful and ineffective. Like eating non-nutritious food, we become hungry again before we know it. Let your rest phases become profoundly effective, and getting back on the trail of life will feel natural. It feels wonderful to get back out there when you are inspired to do so, and after inspiring air in a slow graceful way, emptying your mind and surrendering to rest, you become inspired.

*

Business is no different from skydiving. We pay our money, we take our chances. We point our heads in the direction of optimism, and we trust that we have what it takes. Our faith comes from standing tall in our knowing of who we are. Fear is the enemy within, and relaxing back into hope is the only way forward. Learn your business, trust your wisdom, and enjoy the flow.

*

The quickest way out of fear is to physically relax, and let go of our thinking. The absence of thought is the beginning of something better.

*

You can be pulled forward by your inspiration, rather than being dragged into it by your fear-induced motivation. Fear kicks us from behind, while inspiration draws us forward from the front like a delicious carrot that we will always get if we are patient and persistent in the nurturing of the feeling of our dream of improvement. Joy is a carrot, love is a banquet.

*

Our willingness to tolerate unpleasant emotions as we pound away at a screw with a hammer is what causes us to be less happy that we could be, and far less competent. When you make a commitment to always look for a way to feel as graceful as possible in every moment, the feeling in your gut is more than enough guidance to distinguish the best way from all the other ways.

*

When we are steeped in worry, it is because we have forgotten the feeling of joy and the cosmology of happiness. When we fixate and ruminate on the problem, there is no light at the end of the tunnel because we are not in the same headspace as the solutions. Feeling better comes from dropping the conversation about the problem, and giving our full attention to the solution. Solutions and happiness live in the same place, and if you are worried, you are someplace else.

*

Inner peace is our basic nature, but it is not the basis of human culture. When finding peace becomes more important than what other people might think of us, we will achieve a sustainable personal culture.

*

We all freak out from time to time, when we loop our thoughts that lead to a feeling of helplessness and doom. By choosing to get off these trains of thought, and look for ideas that either solve our problems or simply make us feel better, we can minimize the time wasted in worry. We always have a choice about what we give our attention to, and so we always choose how we feel.

*

When we slow down and find our calm center of balance prior to action, and rekindle the skill within us, everything we do works better. By collecting and focusing our energy, we tap into the part of ourselves that has no resistance to flow, no resistance to grace. When we center ourselves, we become the best version of ourselves.

*

Following an exciting time in the wilderness, the sky, or the sea, notice how you feel. Notice how your whole outlook on life has shifted toward optimism, and your demeanor has softened from your day to day "work" persona. It is as if the stress circuit gets pushed over the edge, and the opponent processes cause us to relax back into our natural wellbeing. We scare ourselves happy.

*

Never procrastinate the communication of appreciation. It is always a priceless opportunity to bump up the vibe, and it is a dish best served hot.

*

The power of outdoor adventures is astounding. By getting out into nature, we change our perspective, and remember who we really are. By challenging ourselves, we create opportunities to impress ourselves.

*

There is no shortage of people who are willing to use any excuse at all to be miserable. You can be sad for them, you can even be angry at them when they point their miserableness at you, but you cannot allow yourself to let go of your freedom to pursue joyous expansion. Nothing matters more than your happiness, and nothing can stop you from feeling the way you want to feel.

*

When we shine our joy, everyone benefits from our happiness. From this perspective, there is no such thing as selfishness. There is only happiness and all that it expands to include.

*

Our expansion is created through experiencing emotional conditions conducive to dreaming a better dream. The worse you feel, the easier it is to realize something that will make you feel better. Contrast is the gift of clarity, and the birthplace of appreciation.

*

Physical fitness makes us a larger container for joy. --Our ability to carry out our dreams is often limited by our level of conditioning, and so expansion of endurance is expansion in possibility.

*

As my wise flight instructor Mike Carpenter taught me, if you lose your engine, nose her down a bit and take a sip of your coffee.

*

Though relaxing into the silent "now", and letting the past drift behind us, we rekindle the spirit of freedom. Clearing out the old, we make room for the new.

*

There is a cozy feeling that takes over when we realize that we are all one tribe. The illusory barriers between us dissolve, and the ways in which we will cooperate and make life better together become illuminated by our warm feeling of oneness. We will unite to soften the worry, and invent a brand-new world.

*

Skydiving safety is partly about attention to detail, partly about emotion, and partly the visualization that knits the two together.

*

Wherever you are, look up. If you feel like crap, work toward feeling a little better. If you feel good, work toward feeling great. If you are feeling absolutely wonderful, look for evidence that feeling wonderful is the key to everything.

*

Fear leads us to thoughts that make us feel lousy. The better the mood, the better the thoughts. When we choose to cheer up by looking in the direction of an improved feeling, we experience the expansion that we wish for.

*

We never benefit from pushing hard against the unwanted. The more attention we give to behaviors and situations that bum us out, the more we step away from our true and powerful nature. We are creating our personal reality either way. Our real power is the focus of our minds, and how we can nurture the feeling of wellbeing by our attention to things that bring us to constructive feeling of joy. When we are vibrating on that frequency, we are incompatible with cranky people, and they simply vibrate out of our experience. Feeling good is always the best defense against feeling bad, and we always choose how we react. How you feel is not their fault, but it is your responsibility.

*

When we continue to breathe beautifully and enjoy the
moment, all of life is yoga.

*

Vibe is everything. The basis of all action is emotion, and the
better we feel, the more skillfully we act as individuals, and
as teams working toward common goals. Create harmony
within your mind and within your teams, and watch the
magic unfold.

*

We know that stress kills. It kills more than cells, it kills
harmony. It breaks down communication between
individuals, who find themselves lost in speed, and
consequently the love level drops. Unless love is in the
house, we are simply not living the good life.

*

When you breathe deeply, and release your resistance, the
way in which everything is going to be OK comes into view.
You cannot see beyond how you feel. Seek better feelings,
find better answers.

*

Few people are willing to admit that they have fear. It is only
the ones who realize it and take it head on that end up

taking the leap of expansion. Fear of danger is just the beginning. It builds our skills of de-escalation so we may take on more consequential matters, like the fear of each other.

*

The old ways are steadily drifting behind us as we move forward into the new paradigm of mutual caring. With each passing day, the number of smiles is increasing, and the number of tears is decreasing. We are waking up, and we are healing. This is so because we chose to make it true.

*

Don't make the dreams that have not yet come true be your excuse to stop dreaming them. Whatever you give our attention to, drifts toward you. Is the absence of your dream your focus of attention, or your dream?

*

Complaining in negative expectation never transformed anyone's life into the alternative to the complaint. That comes from directing the attention toward what helps you lighten up, and onward to the dream that lights your mind on fire just to dream it. Elaborate on what you desire, and clarify how it will feel. Speak aloud of it often, with clear "I

AM" statements. I am creative. I am abundant. I am going to...

*

Have you challenged your illusory boundaries today?

*

A joyful life is a series of joyful moments. Most people miss out on the joyful moments because they are holding out for a joyful life.

*

Inspiration can come from anywhere. Ultimately it is you who chooses to look for it, and the desire for inspiration is the root of wisdom itself. Heroism is daring to look within ourselves to recover our connection to absolute optimism. The brave hope, the heroic believe, the wise know.

*

I have come to the conclusion that coming to conclusions in anything less than a happy state of mind is a very bad idea.

*

Skydiving is the most metaphorically relevant activity in my life. The more I relax and enjoy my experience, the better I fly.

*

Explore what scares you, and you will find that your territory is larger than you have been using thus far. Fearless expansion into our grey zones is how we spread the light within ourselves.

*

Fear is worrying about having enough food to eat. Fearlessness is planting a garden and sharing the produce. Love is productive.

*

Without a plan in the sky, the pilot can get lost. Without a calm pilot, all is lost. Keep breathing, and make everything alright.

*

Humanity is on the way to understanding the power of visualization. Some are learning it by magnetizing the negative possibilities by fixating and worrying, while others are consciously making their most beautiful dreams come true.

*

The feeling of fear is always an indication of where our focus is taking us. The more we fixate on the possibilities that we do not want, the more we are moving in the direction of the undesired experience; thus fear is warranted. Fear is the signal from your higher self saying: "go the other way with your thinking, before it's too late!"

*

Nightmares are just a mirror into the mindset that you have cultivated. Dreams are just an indication of something spinning around in our consciousness. There is no place in the mind that is so subconscious that we cannot change it by persistent attention to the alternative that it is pointing to. Change your persistent focus of attention, and your will change your point of attraction, and the dreams have to change. This makes a very clear case for the eradication of fearful and violent programming in your viewing habits. Garbage in, garbage out.

*

If you can find a way to cheer up, you can find a way to make things better. Optimism shares a bed with happiness, and their lovechild is solution.

*

Danger is the ultimate double-edged sword. One side cuts into comfort and safety, the other side into fear.

*

All we need to do is stop letting the reason for the expansion be our excuse not to expand, and instead get infatuated with the story of what is to come.

*

When we relax and appreciate the beauty around us, we add value to the scenery by being the audience of the Universe. When we bask in the beauty of the people around us, even the hard to appreciate, we add value to our object of attention by shining a spotlight on their positive aspects. We observe the world by looking, we beautify the world by appreciating.

*

Let your happiness grow despite the reasons for fear. Let it expand even though you have not yet fixed everything. Let it roll, let it rock, whether or not anyone else joins in the dance. When you shine despite the darkness, and allow the real you flow forth, you commit the holy act of expanding the universe in your unique and beautiful way. There is no limit to how good this can get when you leave fear behind.

Nobody can hear your music but you, so you might as well dance anyway.

*

Loving each other is the greatest gift we can give to our planet, and to ourselves. In order to advance this world to the next chapter, human kindness will be the core principle that will unite us all. Rather that walking the petty, selfish path of the past, we will go the only route that ever would have worked. We will let kindness inspire expansion, and take care of every last soul.

*

Peace is home. Silence is the way in which peace flows back in. Every Master who walked the earth discovered the pregnancy of the void, as every simple man finds solace in the peaceful silence of simple action. We need not go to Tibet, because Tibet is always inside us. All we need to do is stop and listen to the silence.

*

Although a negative emotional response is a very sane reaction to observing unwanted circumstances, no problem was ever solved by continuing to look in the direction of the problem. By making an about-face and looking toward the alternative to the undesirable, we become the solution-oriented powerful creators that we were meant to be.

*

You know you are in the process of identifying solutions by the feeling of relief that flows into your soul.

*

As our circle of loved ones grows, our fear grows alongside our love. If love is to remain unlimited by fear, we must surrender to fearless trust. True bravery always knows the reasons for fear, but chooses to focus in the direction that is most beneficial despite the risks. We cannot control who goes and when, but we can love them as they are, right there, right now.

*

There is nothing more beautiful than human compassion. When we fearlessly allow love to turn into action, we become who the Universe needs us to be.

*

Have you ever felt like the luckiest person in the world?

*

I have never felt more alive than after I thought I was going to die. This is how life flows back in for me, through appreciation spurred by contrast. When I realize everything is going to be OK, and allow that deep sigh of relief, I return to my inspired, appreciate nature. Thankfully, my life is full of the gifts of fear that refresh my love of life in this way. If we remember this feeling, we no longer need to scare ourselves sane.

\*

Nobody performs well when their heart is beating too fast. The brain channels resources from higher cognitive processes to the save your ass at all costs mindset, in order to escape the worst-case scenario. The best-case scenario is not in the house. If you slow down your heart a little bit, you have access to all that you are, which is brilliant, insightful, and capable of great things. If feeling as good as possible becomes your primary goal, everything else takes care of itself.

\*

We can only attract thoughts that mirror the feeling tone of where we are at the moment, and so if we want to raise our vibe from a place of fear, we must be more general in our attention so that the wellbeing that is natural to us can flow back in due to the subsiding of our resistance. By feeling better, we attract better feeling thoughts. Better soil, better plant.

*

Peace of mind is always available to those who are willing to sit in silence. Content always draws us into the feverous drama of life, while silence always brings us back to center. Whatever is tripping you out, try putting it down for a while, and allow the blissful feeling of relief in. Breathe and just be, and you will see that your basic nature of peace always sits waiting for your open mind.

*

We have a job to do and fear has nothing to do with it. We must look into our hearts and find compassion. We must look into the soil and bring forth nutritious food. We must look at the environment and promote ecological balance. We must look into the future and see the improvement that our lives have been generating through our experience, and know that it is coming. Fear is irrelevant. Let's get to work.

*

A starving farmer feeds no one. Take care of yourself too.

*

When you are bumming out, it is because you are focusing on something that makes you unhappy, so go general. When you are in joy, it is because you are focusing on something that makes you happy, so get more specific. Smell the flowers and pet the puppy dogs, and appreciate the wellbeing that is everywhere. Elaborate on what you love and why you love it, and you will notice more of that. Life is a focus game, and your attention creates your experience.

*

The cranky mentality often results in higher management not listening to their subordinates, or asking for their suggestions on how to reduce waste and promote growth. The janitor can offer the key perspective that makes or breaks a company. Wisdom can come from anywhere, and the wise always keep their ears open for the next good idea.

*

We only need to impress ourselves, and the friends we love, of course. Their higher perspective of you brings you to a new place in knowing who you really are. Our loved ones make us better by adding their loving perception to our concept of ourselves. What do your friends love about you? What do they know you can do if you expand beyond your fear, and into the magnificence that you are? Listen to their love.

*

Know that the better life you have been dreaming of is coming into being, and that the best times are still ahead. Hoping that this is the truth moves you in the right direction, but you will not arrive at the destination until hope is upgraded into belief. It is the knowing with no outward evidence that creates a true visionary creator.

*

Thank you fear and anger, for your clarifying darkness. You show me who I am by touring me through what I am not. The not-way shows the way.

*

When we are in a low state of mind, and someone tells you to just take a deep breath and smile, you want to tell them to shove it. I get that. It is just too far away from where you are to work for you. Rather than judging, and finding fault, we are always better served by simply turning in the direction of whatever makes us feel better. It an idea presented by a loved one chaps your ass at first, withdraw your defenses and let it in. If we know that we aren't perfect, we must be coachable.

*

It is natural to believe that the physical world is all there is, especially when you are experiencing intense suffering. Keep an open mind and a softened heart. Take a moment to relax into petting your cat, listening to children laugh, or watching the birds fly. When you slow down and make yourself open to new ideas outside your certainty, these words will make sense to you. Be easy about all of this. Even "real" problems are just tiny issues when we take into account the larger perspective. When we remember the inevitability of physical end, and just enjoy the ride for what it is, we can lift our spirits to the place where we have come from, the eternal nature of the mind. The feeling-place of our infinite nature is our original happiness; they are one and the same. Settle your soul into the immortality of joy, and ongoing nature of consciousness that is who you truly are. There is no need to wait and see what happens after your form no longer functions to feel this as true. You are a mind that needs no form, and whatever happens here in the three-dimensional world is a fleeting story in the epic journey of your soul's experience.

*

Although we have many goals in life, there is one main objective that we all seem to share: "Whenever possible, it is my desire that I enjoy myself." When you remember that we are all on the same trip, it is easy to love each other.

*

Your heroic compassion is needed. The technological world is now spinning so fast that our humanity has been left behind. Our minds have become as sharp and quick as our technology, and now it is our hearts that require expansion. Through our empathy without judgment, we can be part of the solution.

*

The fear of feeling and expressing appreciation and love is the only thing that can prevent us from experiencing all the joy that life has to offer. When you bravely charge into your world with love as your shield, nothing can stop you, and so there is nothing to fear. Your greatest gift is your ability to allow love to flow through you, and into your world. Love gets us through everything that this world presents us. This is because the events of your life were skillfully crafted by your soul for the purpose of your expansion into love. If you take any other road, you will get lost in an unloving perception, and you will lose the lesson. It's always about love.

*

We have to give love to get love. When we give love without being attached to whether or not it is returned, we are walking the good path. It is attachment to outcome that separates the human mind from the Divine. Be love, and accept all as it is.

We are amazing when we are having fun. Everything we touch turns to gold when we are in our highest state of mind, and so reaching for the best feelings we can get our hands on just makes good sense.

*

If you are feeling scared about something, it is usually because you have not made all the necessary preparations, both physical and mental. If you are worried about getting hurt in skydiving, for example, learn how to land your parachute better, in a diverse set of circumstances. With only a few simple steps, you are on your way to feeling better. Ignorance is not bliss, preparation is. Remember, safety is no accident, it is deliberate.

*

There are plenty of bad endings in our past to suggest worry. It is the possibility of good endings in the future that drives us to take the next step through fear. The visualization process of positive unfolding is not only a distraction from the negative visualization, it a dress rehearsal for the desired outcome. Worry doesn't help, but mental preparation most certainly does.

*

I have realized that my life is about the seeking and finding more things to love, and milking the love that I have already found. As fear squeezes my intensions, it creates a contrasting backdrop that illuminates the joy when I return to its loving embrace. Keep looking for what you are wanting to find, and put your past behind you. Fear is based on a past that no longer exists, unless you want to dig it up and make it real again.

It is normal to experience emotional reactions based on past experiences. That is called learning. If, however, we want to experience something different from the past, we must accept that this is a novel situation. You must dare to consider the possibility that things will unfold differently, and far better than before. Being hopeful and expectant of success is a powerful form of bravery.

*

The limitations and constraints that we encounter are fabrications of mind, and all we need to do is change our perspective and we are free again. No one can ever take away your capacity to dream bigger, not even your doubt.

*

Attention to the stories of the past will only serve to bring your past into your present. The past is just a parable of who you used to be, and now your job is to become infatuated with the vision of what is to come. There is no fate when it comes to your personal reality. Collective fate is cooperative effort that amasses a tremendous amount of belief in a great many souls who expect a certain experience. As Neil Donald Walsh stated in "Conversations with God"; fate is From All Thoughts Everywhere. As part of the collective consciousness of humanity, your steps towards the New Earth are significant. Many others are also dreaming of this fate. Hold the new loving world clearly in your mind, and it begins to come into form. It is not destiny, it is choice.

*

Your ability to appraise the situation is inversely proportional to the speed of that situation. Your gut always tells you that something isn't right, but you need to be moving slowly inside, and with awareness, if you are to make the necessary course corrections when things are headed in a direction that might end badly. Slow down your thoughts and examine their veracity and preferability, and keep thinking your way to the best-case scenario.

*

Nurture your inner pilot, with the flow that comes along with self-trust. You have experienced many massive victories in life, and when you review this list, you reconnect with your true nature.

*

Have you been noticing all that you want to be different about this world, or are you looking for the positive aspects that fill you with joyful appreciation? Can you feel the expanding wellbeing of this beautiful planet? Things are not broken, but they are expanding. Harmony naturally unfolds if we get out of the way.

*

Your best is being born out of your worst, uncovered by your self appreciation, and reburied by your fear and doubt. Celebrate your shining moments, and do not dwell on your past, and you will expedite the natural process that unearths your inner best.

*

We fear uncertainty, and yet there is always something we can do to ease our concerns. Even when there is nothing we can physically do to change the situation right now, rather than worry and indulge in negative visualizations, we can always focus our efforts on slowing down our respiration, and reaching for the best feeling thought from where we are. Relief is always just one deep breath away.

*

There is a universal energy that herds all experience to itself. We live our lives, explore the many details of our experience, and we find over and over that the grand design is such that we eventually figure out that love really is the answer. Fear is the only thing that can hold us back from realizing its true power, but we must grant it power over us through our fixations to thoughts that bring us down. Collect the lessons and think of them fondly, so that you can see yourself the way the Angels see you. You are loved far beyond your comprehension.

*

We fear when we do not feel in control in what we perceive to be a serious situation. Given the truth that our expectations profoundly skew our experiences, the feeling of control over our minds makes us feel more secure. A sensation of safety is the next logical step when we realize the power of the mind.

*

While we are lost in our busy adult world, the rest of the planet is celebrating. The animals and children are playing, the plants are growing, the waves are lapping on the seashore. Will you find a moment to look up from your hamster wheel and rejoin the party?

*

What a wonderful world this is. It all leads to better, and the worst things appear to be, the better they ultimately can become. Without challenge, we do not benefit from the expansion into the new idea. We live, we learn, we create a better possibility from what we have lived and learned. Perfect.

*

We get out-of-sorts over so many things, but when we realize that our negative emotion is not really about the topic itself, but our attention to the problem rather than the solution, we realize that our emotional experience is completely within our control.

All we need to do is stop letting the reason for the expansion be our excuse not to expand.

*

We need a plan if we are to negotiate danger. On the other hand, we also need to be adaptable, and the part of the plan that makes this possible is: "When in doubt, slow down and breathe". If you can't get your brain back, you can't fix anything

Taking ownership of problem is how we inspire the answers, but taking ownership of the solutions, and ignoring the fact that they aren't in physical manifestation just yet, this is how we become compatible with the new and improved reality. We have to let go of the problem mentality if we are to get in the proximity of the solutions. We must take the mental bounce into the better conditions that are cued up by the realizations about our experience.

We come from a long line of problem illuminators, and we are now beginning a new line of solution highlighters. The old way was to incessantly describe and complain about what needs to be fixed about the world. The new way is to pivot on the problems and give our full attention to the story of the alternative. We create the content of our minds' place of dwelling, and therefore it is profoundly wise to dwell on the desired creation.

*

The fear of standing out leads us to hold back our most beautiful essence from the world. Being your true self, with all of its unique inspiration, defies normalcy in the most splendid ways. You are not here to be the same as those who have come before. You are here to fearlessly expand the IS with your magnificent distinctiveness.

*

The now is as fresh and open as we allow it to be. The infinite positive possibilities are all cued up, all we need to do is let go of the past, and allow ourselves a feeling a relief so that the past can be left behind. We then just open our eyes and see a new world.

If you aren't having fun, you aren't doing it right, and you shouldn't be doing it until you feel the joy. The inner emotional guidance system is flawless. If you do not feel good moving forward, you are not yet ready. It may not be a "no", but a "not yet". Resistance is most often a program within the mind, a belief that causes doubt. It may be clarifying that you have more to do to prepare, or it might be the bully in your mind that doubts your worthiness in all moments. This voice is the "inner critic", and it is not you. It is a ghost of all the doubters who threw shade upon your beautiful soul, and if you do not pass the microphone to the bully, you can hear your true guidance. Not feeling good about the content of your mind must make you curious about the origins of your emotion. Wonder about the source of an idea that makes you feel powerless, and explore its veracity. It is true? Is it loving? Is it connecting and liberating and creative? If the answer is no, swipe left and look for a new thought that is true for you.

*

I think that all the world's suffering and confusion could easily be softened if each one of us would just take five minutes a day to go sit on a rock and smile. You do not need a guru outside of yourself, because if you know how to listen, that voice speaks to you with guidance specific to your journey. The voice of truth knows your name. It sees your journey and it knows your value. All you need to do is become quiet inside and listen.

*

We do not need to be afraid of hurricanes and earthquakes, we need to prepare. We need to store some basic supplies, and if the power goes out and there are disruptions in the trucking, we need to band together and have potluck suppers, and sing happy songs together in the darkness. When we remember that we are not alone, and we shed the fear of each other, there is no place for fear to hide within us.

Fearless cooperation is the best answer to our biggest fears.

*

Nothing empowers a person more than doing the right thing, for the right reasons. While the force necessary to paddle up a river is great, when we point downstream, we are supported in ways we cannot fully understand. Being good is grace, because this Universe is conspiring in all moments to bring love to light.

When we set sail for a life with deeper meaning, we are always in for a glorious journey of epic proportions. Purpose gives us a meaning to live. Higher Purpose gives us a reason to expand. Meaning always puts the wind at our backs.

*

Your higher self is absolutely fearless. This is not because it doesn't see the dangers. It is because your higher self always sees the solutions that your present moment has made clear. The better-than-this alternative is what the best version of you is all about.

*

Appreciation is an appropriate word for what a highly experienced skydiver experiences when waiting to jump. We appreciate the clouds and are thankful for the sky. We notice the other skydivers alongside us in the airplane and appreciate their enthusiasm. The fact that they too appreciate the value of this amazing experience is what bonds us together, and creates the collective magic that causes safety. We bask in the glow of our moment, and enjoy being exactly where we are. Apply this to everything.

*

What if every time someone who cares for you reminded you to take a deep breath, you simply did it because it leads in the direction of an improved feeling? When your goal is to be as happy as possible, anything that gets you there is a welcome signpost directing you where you originally wanted to go. Do not resist assistance and insight. We are one in our desire for wellbeing, and when we realize this, we let their intention for our ease and flow enter our minds without the resistance of the ego mind. We support each other, because we are each other.

*

You have memories of your errors, the moments when you chose in a way that clarified how you will choose differently next time. That was you, playing the role of not you, learning who you want to be in the future. You expand you by exploring not you.

*

It is far easier to think great thoughts when we feel great. This is because when we are happy, we are being true to our inner nature, and the genius that we really are takes charge of our minds. Joy is a cornucopia of insight, the portal to brilliance.

*

The fear-driven can only continue the inertia of the world as it is, or possibly make things worse for themselves. It is the brave who will ignore doubt and ridicule and do whatever is necessary to make things better.

We are both the fear driven cranky person and the loving celebrator of it all. Remembering this as often as possible seems to skew the percentages, leaving us happier than many of the people around us. Embrace your every aspect as a part of yourself. Do not feel shame for experiencing fear and anger, it is part of your mind. Like a house with many rooms, your mind has places that you do not wish to linger, but love them you must. Love all of what you are, because what you resist, persists.

*

The sooner we remember to breathe, the less we tend to overreact. Fear is just intensity without respiration.

*

While life will continue to put you in the back seat with shock and awe, it is a wise person who relishes the inevitable expansion that comes from these moments. Accept the truth of what is, and notice how much of your experience is subject to interpretation. It is a big hairy deal, or just a passing storm cloud?

*

Each of us is on the path from fear to love in a vast array of subjects. As we each clarify our preferences and become congruent with them, our planet migrates from sadness to joy, from anguish to peace, and from selfishness to compassion. We really are evolving, and everything really is going to be alright.

This is the time of ascension, and the transition is quite a show. Know where you are going so you don't get stuck in between gears. Our planet was in 3D, the vibration of suffering and separation from the miraculous nature of the Universe. Our observation of the undeniable weirdness of the world brings us up into 4D, the transition zone between 3D and 5D, the place of Heaven on Earth. We are on our way to a collective experience of love, and depending on which way we gaze, we can live in the all-pervasive love of the New Earth, or cause our vibration to drop back down to the way we were. Which world do you choose?

*

You don't need to fix everything right now. You just need to improve your end of the world. Start with how you feel in this moment, and take your personal journey gradually up the scale of emotions, and see how your improved attitude transforms the world around you. One step up the emotional ladder at a time, we climb our way up to the Light.

*

We have a choice in every situation: cheer up or suffer the consequences.

*

We have to meet people in the emotional vicinity of where they are. If someone is despondent, we cannot reach out to them through joy and elation, because they cannot yet hear that frequency. We must gradually and gracefully bring them up to anger, frustration, and then hope, and finally point them in the direction of belief in the feeling of worthiness. Remind them that they are loved and accepted, and the kindle the knowledge that they are blessed. It will be necessary to draw their attention from the unwanted reality to allow a feeling of relief, in any way that lifts the feeling of helplessness to hope. We all have to surrender to the unchangeable, and find a way to be happy anyway, regardless of the situation. As a loving guide, you can help those who are willing to receive assistance. Some are not, and to them we give our loving blessing, and wait for them to be ready.

*

The consequences of miserableness are more experiences that feel similar to how we feel. We are drawing into our experience the conceptual equivalent of what we are dwelling on. It is therefore wise to dwell on the desired experiences and their complimentary emotions. You will create either way.

*

The you that has been thus far been has demonstrated is just a shadow of the you that is on the way. There is emotional inertia to contend with, and doubt happens. Give your full attention to the expanded version of you, and it will come into being that much faster. In truth, the full you is already in existence, waiting for you to walk your path in a more joyful way.

*

Slower is smoother. Smoother is easier. Easier is less resistance. Less resistance always feels better. Feeling better is our emotional intelligence telling us we are on the right path.

*

There is never a good time to panic. Yes, there are times when serious situations arise, but that is definitely not a good time to panic. Breathe deep, focus on where you want the situation to go, and surrender to enjoying the process of making your vision into reality. Proceed slower, smarter, and with your full awareness. Your improved mood is all you need to get through this.

*

How is your breathing right now? Is there room for further expansion? How big is your heart right now? Is there room for expansion there too? Be more of what you are.

*

When fear and anger take control of a situation, the flow of essential communication breaks down. When we see this happening, we must take a moment to reconnect with our original happiness, and then return to the all-important task of harmoniously cooperating with our team. We really do need each other.

*

Most people seem mentally focused on just getting through the day; doing the bare minimum and preventing bad things from happening. When we are spending our time considering what might go wrong, we are not visualizing the ways in which things might go really well, and preparing for that. Glance at the negative alternatives, and ask yourself: "what would be the opposite of that?", and then get into the expansion of that vision.

*

Dangerous things do not always go according to plan. When complex situations arise, the optimistic person will ultimately have the means to persevere, and create solutions in the moment. Hopeful happiness will always be the best defense against danger.

*

In between terror and boredom is the place called adventure, where we are able to blossom into our highest potential. Without doing things that scare us in some way, we are floating leaves on a still pond, going nowhere.

*

The inertia of joy is so powerful that if we spend most of our time there, and get addicted to the feeling, our emotional buoyancy allows us to flow easily through challenging times. When we become hooked on feeling great, not only do we transcend difficulties, we radiate a wave of intentionality that precedes us in life.

We glide on the lift of joy.

*

When you ponder the significance of profound truth, changes almost always become necessary to the way you have been thinking and living. Let truth change you.

*

When we flow in expertise, we simplify ourselves. We focus so exclusively that we lose ourselves in the beauty of the experience of skill in motion. This is when we leave fear behind, and move forward without resistance. Skill is flowing joy.

*

Our failures ring true only as long as we toll the bell of their story, but our moments of greatness ring out into eternity. The crest of the wave called you just gets higher and higher. You are the high watermark of your experiences, nothing less.

*

The pursuit of mastery within the realm of risk is where we stoke the fire of the human spirit.

*

A life with too much risk is often too short, but a life without risk is no life at all.

*

One cannot simultaneously prepare for the worst-case scenario and the best-case scenario. One mindset is fixed on preventing something, while the other is focused on creating something. By spending most of our time practicing and preparing for things to go smoothly, we increase the likelihood of great things happening for us.

*

The present version of you is the only version that matters, because that is where all your pulling power is. Place your awareness on your infinite potential in this moment. The real you is elated, passionate, eager, and filled with the joy of being alive. If you find that these words do not apply to the present-moment version of you, there is some work to do. It is time to tune your instrument to make the music sound better to your heart. Remembering who you are is the key to happiness.

*

Abbreviated Owner's Manual for the mind: If you are not enjoying the thoughts that are in your head, change them, before they change you. You are what you think.

*

You are not just seeing a perfect skydive with a soft landing, you are picturing YOU being the one making that beautiful landing. Cast yourself in the leading role of a story that ends really, really well.

*

Selflessness without an ounce of selfishness appears to be a dead-end street. Take care of yourself as you take care of your world. If you are not able to fly, how can you uplift anyone?

We have been taught to be humble. We have been taught that it is holy to be meek. We have also been taught that we were created in the image of the Divine, the All-That-IS in all Its glory. Both things cannot be true. If we are to be true to our creative blueprint, we must know who we are. We are grand. We are creative. We are brilliant beyond measure. We are here to love all the world, and part of that world is you.

The Universe of which you are a holographic creation dearly wants you to love yourself. That isn't selfish, it is natural.

*

Fear says: "Better safe than sorry." The flip side is, sacrificing the adventure of life to avoid all danger is not living free. From a certain perspective, living in fear is not living at all. The world is waiting to be expanded through your exploration of possibility. Freedom always requires a moderate level of risk. Nothing risked, nothing gained. To paraphrase one of our wisest American forefathers, Benjamin Franklin, those willing to trade freedom for safety deserve neither.

\*

Breathe Deep. Think Deep. You can't have one without the other.

\*

Appreciating the beauty of your time and place is the doorway to becoming a realized being. The fullness of who you are cannot come into your awareness until you notice how very lucky you are to be alive.

\*

Start by asking: "in my best moments, who am I?" Trust that the wisdom teachers who will benefit you will come when you clarify who you are.

\*

Withholding your happiness or your love in order to make a point or change the behavior of another simply costs too much. There will always be situations that are not to your liking, but sacrificing your happiness is not an effective means to any end.

*

Remember your amazing moments, the times that your external world was congruent with your inner world. The experiences that we savor are a clear indication of our true nature, and a signpost for what we desire to experience again. Expand consciously in the direction of yourself.

*

Upliftment is always a two-sided arrangement. On one hand there are the words aimed at the improvement of one's outlook, on the other is the willingness of the receiver to truly let it in. Deservingness is ultimately a self-imposed condition.

**Read these words aloud:**

# I am worthy.

Do you immediately allow the feeling, or does your mind present resistance to acceptance? It is a true statement, but the mind defends its enculturated perspective. The ego mind is the voice of all insecurity, and it shies away from feeling worthiness and pride in who we are. This was programmed by a culture that is misguided to believe that we were born in original sin, and any virtues we demonstrate appear as a result of teachings. This is false. You are worthy because of who you basically are. You were made of love, by love, for love, and believing anything else is a delusion that keeps you small. To feel worthiness, one must look within, with eyes wide open to the light that you are.

*

Settle down.

Drift gently into the grace of glide, the breath that flows. Soften your urgency and find peace in the not needing to get it all done right this red hot minute. Just be right here, right now, at ease.

You must become more often in this experience of the bliss of true peace, we all must. If you are to sustain this journey with its long windy road of bizarre truths, we must become more skilled in collecting our minds. These truths must first be realized in a wakeful mind, and then acted upon. This is the path of the awakening soul, coming to know itself.

But for now, in this moment, rest your weary head and lay your mind back into the peaceful recline of forgiveness. If we are to experience the enlightened perspective, we are required to release attachments to all of the drama in our minds, absolutely of all of it...even that thing that your mind just spouted as an exception. Set it all down in this moment and just be. Don't make that thing more important than your brilliant sanity, grounded in inner peace. There are no small upsets. There is only peace and not-peace.

Nothing in this world is worth severing your connection to the Divine mind within you, the emotional context of peace without separation. Oneness is a healing of the mind. When we allow both perspectives of any dynamic as valid and part of a wholeness, the partnership is seen for the value that it presents as a unique knowing of what it is to be human. Taste and distaste are part of one thing, clarifying with light and contrasting lack of light, what the world is and how we wish it to be. This is the perfection of all our experiences when we stand outside of judgment of good and bad. We live and we learn, and through the expansion, we refine the common goal of any kind and just society, informed by the non-dualistic wisdom of Oneness.

*

Your mind has a basis beyond your understanding. Your consciousness is your knowing that you are, just like everyone else. This point of focus is specific, and your experiences through this lens has created the unique persona that you define as self. Look beneath this self, to the origin of your mind. This awareness is an inseparable aspect of the quantum field, and it is connected to the Akash that comprises all that is. The basis of your awareness is the same as everybody else, everything else in the Universe. We are all made from the same stuff.

When you gaze into the eyes of another, look beyond the physical body, the storyline and the personality that has been created from consciousness being in that experience. They are you, in them. This is the realization of Oneness, the Unity consciousness that comprises all that is. You are a Divine Spark of the One Mind, holy and sacred, as is that pain in the ass neighbor that you keep thinking as separate from you.

*

The reward for a deep slow breath is the feeling of relief that has been at the root of every pursuit that takes our breath away.

Awe is accessible right here, right now.

*

Love illuminates, while fear creates the dark contrasting background that makes love shine more brilliantly. In the end, even fear serves love.

*

Mood matters more than probability. Without the connection to the wisdom of your higher self, the world is a very dangerous place. A fearful mood skews probability toward the unwanted visualization. A joy-filled mind, expecting one's leverage over matter, will not see obstacles ahead, but the open spaces between things. Life is not a roll of the dice, it is the product of how we feel in that moment.

Being ready for risk is about maintaining your emotional buoyancy, so that you can see the world through the eyes of your best self.

*

When you have turned your parachute too low, and are diving at the earth, do not scream NO! at the ground, Sing YES! to the horizon. Fighting against something unwanted is not the same thing as nurturing the alternative.

*

Hope must be rekindled. We do this by playing in the mindscape of the image of the improved future. It is through our enjoyment of the visualization that we crystallize our positive experience. We live it because we become it.

*

Ultimately, it is the intended future that really matters to the powerful creative mind, fixated on the New Earth. Over-attention to current conditions points us away from where we would prefer things go. Focus your attention on the better possibilities, and those experiences increase in probability. Creation is deliberate, intentional delusion to look for what you are wanting to see.

*

Feeling like a winner is how we become compatible with winning.

*

Worrying is like stepping on the accelerator pedal and the clutch at the same time. There's lots of heat and noise, but no forward progress. Reduce your RPM, engage your gears, and smoothly move toward solutions to your concerns.

Relax, Focus, and Flow.

*

If you feel eagerness and hope, you are in connection to the real you, and you are on your way to better. If you are feeling lethargic apathy, you are focusing in a way that the real you would not, and the opposite of improvement is on its way to you. The mental frequency that leads to all constructive creation always feels better than the one that leads away from improvement. Let your gut be your GPS.

*

Worry is just hope pointed in the wrong direction.

*

When I am glad to be alive, the little things shine as brightly as the big ones, and I bask in the joyous possibilities of what is to come.

*

In easy times, we must prepare for challenge. Likewise, when we are in difficult times, we must prepare for celebration. Flowing brilliance requires positive expectation, and it is possible for the creative mind to conjure a world completely unlike the one it is experiencing. Creation is based on imagination.

*

When we let go of our need to be right about what is wrong with the world, we return to the feeling of grace that nurtures the positive mindset that leads to improvement. Cheering up is always the first step toward sustainable positive change.

*

We all freak out a bit when it comes to dangerous things, but that doesn't have to mean we have to take the bait. Fear can simply be a bit of static in the background while we remain focused on where we want to go, and why we want to go there.

*

More love, less fear: go big or go home alone.

*

Inner silence and focus is a prerequisite for skillful execution, as is a profound appreciation for the joy of the experience. Therefore, peace and love really is the answer to all challenges.

*

We often think of safety as the absence of danger, when in fact safety cannot exist without danger. When we consciously creep toward the edge of control, we create the flowing experience that is risk very little danger. This is the place where skill skews probability, and we experience our power over the material world. Without risk, there is no heroic expansion.

*

Wisdom is foresight born in hindsight.

*

In several aspects of our experience, metaphorically speaking, we all have toilet paper hanging off our shoes. Without our friends, we will never know everything that we need to know to avoid embarrassment and dangerous failure. The overwhelming field of information that we need to keep track of requires many eyes and ears, which is why life is a team sport.

*

To be a great skydiver, you've got to surrender to loving the experience. Allow gravity to have its way with you, and you can fly. If you apply this to your most passionate inspiration, it is even more true.

*

Although fear may occasionally put you in the back seat, the only way to regain control is to lean forward into the experience. Joy is skill, love is mastery.

*

Read this aloud, if you dare:

I wish to stop once again and look upon the world.

I wish for my eyes to be made new, so that the world's true colors are visible to me.

Make my ears new again, so that I may hear the brilliant sounds of nature in their true form.

I wish to know with new knowing that all is well.

271

I wish to release all suspicion of love's dark side, so that I may love more authentically all beings in all moments.

*

Learning from fear is essential for our survival. Dwelling on the object of fear, on the other hand, is incredibly dangerous.

*

If you want more of it, talk more about it. If you want it to go away, let it go, and pay attention to something else. This is not ignorance; it is conscious creation of your future.

*

Incessantly speaking of things that we do not like is called complaining. Incessantly speaking of things that we like is called appreciating. To appreciate is to expand and add value to something. We are drawing more attention to a facet of our reality that we desire to experience again, and so are paving the way for this to happen.

*

Be joyful in the darkness, and sing songs of the light.

*

The rule of law must never take precedence over the rule of the heart. Mercy is moral. Grace is just. Love is guidance.

*

My many near death experiences have been the pivot points that have launched me into a greater appreciation of life. I am not suggesting that we seek out brushes with death, but when they find us, we inevitably expand into the fullness of our true nature. Our Love of Life is illuminated by the contrasting background created by nearly exiting the material realm. Thankfully, a mind skilled in imagination can experience the same contrast that awakens your joy for being alive. You can remember who you are and what you came here to do, and infuse the rest of your journey with greater meaning, based on your values. Bring forth more of yourself into this life experience, because even though your soul lives forever, this body does not.

*

The experiences that repulsed you, infuriated you or terrified you are the launching place into a new possibility. They were powerful for you due to their relevance to your unique journey, that is why you felt personally triggered. These experiences clarify what you want, and help you to find appreciation when you get there. We knew that this was the case when we signed on, and so rising up from complaint to eagerness to make things better is the natural consequence of powerful emotional negativity. It is knowledge of your personal truth. Be thankful for the guidance, and embark on the new journey.

*

We are all born enlightened and fearless, but we become trained into the lower vibrations by people and experiences, and we draw limiting conclusions about ourselves. Returning to our true nature is the task at hand, the unlimited child within us. We do this by following the path of our joy, and letting go of the past as we relax into the flow of our bliss. In the glide that is fearless joy, we find access to insight from a much larger pool of wisdom within.

*

When we get intense, we force things and lose our grace and flow. If we realize we are speeding up and tightening down, and choose to relax a bit and look for beauty, we reconnect with our skill.

Struggle does not lead to skill; only ease and flow grounded in appreciation will lead to the demonstration of your magnificence.

*

Being afraid is a part of being alive. Focusing exclusively on avoidance what we are afraid of is how we rob ourselves of experiencing all that life has to off us. Take fear head on, slowly and methodically, and see how big you can be when you forget that you were afraid.

*

When we punish others, we vibrate with an emotional frequency that feels terrible, and thus we find more and more reasons to complain. We see the world through the eyes of our mindset. When we praise others, our way of focusing causes unforeseen positive effects to play out. Through our attention to the favored aspects, we rendezvous with more to be praised and appreciated.

*

Fear narrows our focus of attention, and therefore our scope of possibilities. It is a myopic view that fixates on whatever is provoking our feeling of insecurity. Relax into the expanded perspective, and look for the many ways that things can get better. There is only one version of crashing, and many versions of flying. Liberate yourself from fear by freeing your mind to see the many ways in which this can go well.

*

When you make your emotional experience contingent on what others say and do, you are a victim of the world. This is because whatever plot-momentum in your immediate surroundings was already in play, now becomes your experience. When you decide that you are going to look for what you are wanting to see to nurture the feeling of who you really are, you are fast on your way to living the life you prefer. You set your own stage, and write your own plot, and create your personal reality. Let people be as they are, and choose to continue your journey toward your preferences despite what they are living. Attention to your own preferences will lead you to arrive within striking distance of your dreams. You intersect with the happiest, most fulfilled version of you when you figure out who you are, and what you want to do. It has nothing to do with anybody else.

*

Some will try to dissuade you from moving forward into your dreams for yourself, and it will be easy to let this get you down. Who cares what someone else says? You must remember that you are deeply in love with your dream.

If you dream of an adventure, that is who you are in that embodiment of your life force energy. If you look to others to nurture this dream or the good feeling it brings you, you are not going to hold on to it for long. This is your vision and only you can nurture and sustain it. Write about the possibility, and speak of it often, to friends and aloud to yourself. You are not alone, you hear you. The Universe hears you. All the physical matter that coalesces to show your dream to you is a cooperative component that is willing and able to manifest what you desire to experience. Firstly, however, you must maintain your conscious emanation of this possibility. You must kindle your dream through knowing that it is true, in premanifested form.

KNOW who you are.

KNOW where you are going.

KNOW that you are worthy.

It is the vision within that is real. The manifestation outside you is just a transitional reality that is reflecting your past vibrational emanation. Ignore the "NOW" enough to focus on the "could be", and eventually it will be. If you merely focus only on the way things are, the present "truth", the dream will never become a reality until you change your focus.

*

Be light about all of this. Appreciate the ride, every aspect of it. Each event clarifies your desire, and each event points you more specifically toward what you really want. There are no wrong turns, because the journey never ends. All you need to do is look where you want to go and keep steering your mind based on what feels best to you.

The Law of Attraction is truth, however even a powerful creator discovers from time to time that what is wanted is not always desirable from another perspective. You may focus and manifest a fast car and then crash it if that is what is in the best interest of your soul's expansion into understanding. You are guided and your experience will always lead you to know better what is ultimately in your best interest on your journey toward the meaningful experiences that you desire. Enjoy your power of manifestation, but remain unattached to the outcome. Be fluid and flexible and seek the deeper meaning behind all the events of your life. When it comes right down to it, what we desire to attract is not money or power or even safety, it is the yearning for insights that bring more light into our souls. We experience so we can more fully understand who we are.

*

The human voice expressing sound reason is the most powerful tool for justice of all. When we listen, we honor clarity within others, and thus we become open to reason from all directions. Many people see wisdom within themselves, but it is a truly wonderful thing when someone sees wisdom in everyone.

*

What if following your path lead you back to liking yourself more than you have thus far allowed? Most of us withhold our rewards in order to light some sort of fire of discontent under our butts. We think that a good whipping will get us off the floor, moving toward improvement. As far as I can tell, it is the other way around. When we allow our self approval in, anything is possible. Notice who you have been when you were kind, when grace took hold of your mind and drove your actions? Notice how it felt at the time, and the ideas and conversations that the feeling led to. Notice the ease with which grace flows within us, and the magic that it creates. This is the experience of connection, congruence with the Divine's wishes for us. It is easy because it is true to our nature to be kind and caring and giving. It is natural to think of the needs of others, and to assist them in the ways that we can. It is graceful to help, because that is the way that the Universe wants us to go.

*

Sometimes we do not have access to happiness, due to the nature of our moment, but we can still find relief. The softening that comes with a feeling of relief points us in the general direction of up, toward happiness. When we are able to return to the full expression of positive emotion, the low we experienced will serve as brilliant contrast to illuminate our appreciation for where we are. In the landscape of the soul, nothing is wasted, it is either growth or it is compost for growth.

*

In a time of terror, a forced smile soon becomes an authentic change of mood. I once tested this in an MRI machine, which is a situation that seriously challenges my fading claustrophobia. I first worked with deep "Ujaia" breathing, or yoga breathing. My heart was still racing. Then I worked to clear my mind. All I could think about was how much I wanted to get free. I kept letting go of the thoughts, and focusing on my breathing. I could not move at all, so graceful yoga movement was out of the question. At this point, I decided to try the "fake it till you make it" method, and work the bottom-up neuro-circuitry, acting the way we wish to feel. Play the part, feel the joy and peace, even if at first you feel like an imposter. It worked like a charm. By halfway through the 45-minute session, I was in a completely different mindset. I was actually able to enjoy the experience, and believe it or not, I was disappointed when it was over. I stopped allowing my preconceived judgment to pave my way to terror, and instead accepted things as they are, and enjoyed myself.

Am I sure it works? Yes I am.

*

Joy is the root cause of all wellbeing: our health, wealth and wisdom all ride in the balance.

*

The enemy of adventure is not danger but laziness. Lethargy works to prevent us from beginning the journey, ands then appears within the adventure in the form of complacency. The lively spark that lights the fire of adventure is awake and aware, thrilled to be in the present moment, alive in the details of the experience.

*

Expansion of the self requires a sort of target fixation on the chosen creation, ignoring all evidence to the contrary. Self-creation, as with happiness, is a matter of tenacious selective perception. Yes, you have and will make mistakes. Yes, you have learned many lessons, and those lessons have made you wise. Forgive your mistakes and find a way to turn this into part of your wisdom training. The ultimate wisdom is knowing oneself, and seeing that you are an integral part of the Divine Cosmos, inventing itself.

*

If we were all judged ourselves by our worst moments, nobody would dare to do anything interesting ever again. Notice, but do not judge. Each experience makes us wiser in a way that could not have been learned without direct experience. There really are no failures on this infinite journey, only realizations of what you are, and what you were and don't want to be again.

*

I find that savoring and rekindling our best moments is a powerful way to create more moments that shine as brightly. I choose to let go of my negative past as much as I can, once I have learned the lesson that the experience taught me. If I do not learn the lesson, it will be presented in a new form until I get with the program. That is the value of the "don't do that again" sort of memory. Once I accept that wisdom as part of myself, however, I absolutely must take a step toward letting the cautionary tale fall by the wayside. The Universe wants you to have the most glorious journey possible toward your enlightened perspective that is the inevitable product of a contemplative life.

*

Sometimes, despite yourself, you succeed. How do you let the good times roll when you don't believe you earned them? Say thank you from the heart and move on. Tip your hat to the timely not-so-random unlikely possibility that drifted graciously toward your favor, and say thank you. You must be grateful and move forward with a feeling of worthiness, because something new is coming and it requires your attention.

The magical glide is facilitated through gratitude. If you are grateful, you own what you reap. Linger in the place of worthiness, make it your home. Stay here in thankfulness, in the authentic faith that things really are going to work out just fine. Trust in the universe. It wants you here. It is the will of the Source of Life that your journey continues onward toward meaning.

*

Joyous inner peace is a gift best served hot. The only way to keep it warm, I have found, is to give it away.

Spread your good feelings, and your best thoughts,

because that's what love does.

*

We all return home, and from the ultimate truth, we never left. The illusion is powerfully convincing, with the enduring nature of suffering on this planet. It helps to remember that nothing we see here has any bearing on the truth of what is. We never left the loving arms of the Divine Parent. It's a pretty intense dream though, and it seems to be taking forever. Look within, beyond the physical shell that the ego has created all around it to feel separate and independent. Look deeper inside, to the I AM under it all. Your feeling of I AM is the same as mine; there is no other. Consciousness is all One. We are all the same Being having countless separate dreams.

Enjoy the illusion of suffering and time while it lasts. It's just a fleeting moment that we created to learn and experience, and it won't last. The real magic is in our ability to make it feel so permanent. We are in fact Source Mind, deluding ourselves into believing that we are Joe Shmo so we can get out of the castle for a bit and pretend we are a commoner. Nothing could be further from the truth, and eventually all truth comes to light.

, ( **INSERT YOUR NAME** ), WILL
HEREBY TRY TO BE THE VERY BEST VERSION OF ME, TO THE VERY
BEST OF MY ABILITY.

IN THIS MOMENT I AM ONCE AGAIN BORN INTO THE FULLNESS OF
WHO I AM.

I WILL HENCEFORTH DO MY VERY BEST TO DREAM INTO
EXISTENCE A VERSION OF ME THAT BRINGS FORTH ALL OF THE
BEST THAT I AM.

I AM CLARIFIED THROUGH ALL THAT I HAVE LEARNED, AND THUS
I WILL BECOME EVEN MORE AWARE OF MY OWN PERSONAL
WISDOM.

I WILL DO MY BEST TO RELISH ALL OPPORTUNITIES TO LEARN
FROM THE WISDOM OTHERS, AND BEAR WITNESS TO THEIR
INFINITE CREATIVE POTENTIAL TO GROW WISER.

I WILL TRY MY BEST TO LOVE MY WAY INTO CONNECTION WITH
OTHERS AND WITH THE DIVINE WHO THEY COMPRISE.

I WILL HONOR THE WAYS OF OTHERS, AND LEARN FROM THOSE
WAYS EVEN WHEN THEY DIFFER FROM MY OWN.

I WILL TRY WITH ALL THAT I AM TO BE THE MOST POWERFUL
POSITIVE FORCE I CAN BE, IN SERVICE TO THE ONE LOVE THAT
UNIFIES US ALL

---

(SIGNATURE)

## Postscript

It is my sincere hope that these well-intended words uplift your vibration in a sustainable manner. May you shine, in your knowing of who you are and what that leads you to love. May you have the courage and faith to be yourself every day of your life, being the happiest most fulfilled version of you. This is my will for you, my fellow human being. I know the light in your eyes and mine is one and the same.

Brian Germain's other books, as of 2025:

Transcending Fear, The Doorway to Freedom

Green Light Your Life: Awakening Your Higher Self

The Parachute and its Pilot: The Ultimate Guide for the Ram Air Aviator

Vertical Journey: The Art of New Age Skydiving

# Here is a handy QR code that leads to Brian Germain's Bookstore and catalogue of services:

Keynote Speaking, Holistic Life Coaching, Nature Therapy Expeditions for Families and Groups, Skydiving Instruction and Advanced Canopy Flight Courses and more.